ARYAN COSTA

Glimpses into an Unscripted Consciousness

Unfiltered. Unbound. Unlearned!

First published by Design Health Labs Ltd. 2026

Disclaimer: The content presented is crafted under a 'nom de plume', Aryan Costa. The wisdom presented herein is purely existential and introspective, derived entirely from personal journey, shaped by lived experience, independent inquiry and self observation, not professional doctrine. Read this as a collection of truths discovered, not rules imposed.

To ensure the reader's experience aligns with the author's deepest clarity of thought, a subtle layer of digital refinement may have been applied to the prose for enhanced grammatical precision and flow. This process was governed by the unwavering commitment to preserve the original voice, philosophical integrity, and creative spirit of the work.

ISBN: 978-9918-0-1552-8

Contents

Foreword

This is not what was first imagined nor is it your typical read. It is what survived decades of doubts, detours, and conversations that almost never made it onto a page. Each page carries traces of those who held up a mirror when looking away would have been easier, who questioned rationale, and who sometimes appreciated the imperfect human behind some of the polished words.

I learned some time ago about '***Runanabhanda***,' a concept found in spiritual traditions that speaks to the body's memory. Not memory as we usually understand it, not recollection or narrative, but memory that lives beneath awareness. It is said to consist of two intertwined forces: genetic memory carried forward through lineage, and the imprint left behind through intimate physical connection. In simple terms, we arrive carrying more than we remember choosing.

Our bodies inherit unresolved patterns, emotional reflexes, fears, longings, and instincts shaped long before language enters the picture. Alongside this, every meaningful physical connection leaves a trace. Not sentimentality, but imprint. A quiet recalibration of the nervous system, the sense of self, the boundaries of trust.

Runanabhanda suggests that much of what we call personality, attachment, aversion, even intuition, does not originate in conscious thought. It originates in stored experience that predates decision. This idea challenges a comforting illusion: that we are blank slates guided primarily by reason. Instead, it proposes that awareness begins in excavation. That clarity comes not from adding more beliefs, but from recognizing what is already embedded.

The reflections that follow are written with this understanding in mind. That much of what we struggle to articulate has already been lived in the body. That confusion is often inherited. That patterns repeat not because we are weak, but because they are remembered somewhere deeper than willpower. This work does not attempt to overwrite those imprints. It attempts to bring them into view. Because awareness is not created. It is uncovered.

No two people meet by accident, and that truth does not depend on the length of the encounter. Even the briefest crossings, a shared glance, a passing conversation, a stranger's kindness, carry an energy that can bend the trajectory of a life in ways the mind may never fully register.

In a single moment, something in us recognizes something in another: a wound, a strength, a fear, a dream we have not yet had the courage to name. That recognition becomes a quiet seed, buried in the subconscious, that later influences decisions, desires, and the stories we tell ourselves about what is possible.

A brief exchange of energy can soften a hardened belief or harden a fragile one. A smile from someone who truly sees us can interrupt a spiral of self-doubt; a harsh word at a vulnerable time can echo for years, shaping what we think we deserve.

Any two people locking eyes across a room may never speak, yet walk away subtly changed, suddenly aware of a longing, an ache, a curiosity that was previously invisible. That fleeting contact can awaken a part of the self that had been sleeping, nudging us toward new paths, relationships, or risks we would never have contemplated without that silent encounter.

These micro-moments accumulate, forming an invisible architecture beneath our choices. A stranger's unwavering presence in a moment of crisis may teach us that help exists; a brief but honest conversation may give us language for something we've felt all our lives; a single act of tenderness may become the reference point for what we will later recognize as love.

We rarely trace these threads back to their source, yet they inform what we pursue, what we avoid, who we trust, and how boldly we step into our own life. In this way, even the shortest meeting is not a passing incident, but a subtle negotiation with fate that shapes the road ahead in ways far beyond what we consciously perceive.

Between those moments and the lives they quietly sculpt, there is a pause we almost never examine. It is the space where habits harden into beliefs, where borrowed expectations begin to feel like personal choice, and where repetition masquerades as destiny.

Over time, these invisible agreements become routines of thought and behavior, so familiar that questioning them feels unnecessary, even dangerous. What begins as influence slowly calcifies into identity, until the path ahead seems fixed not by intention, but by silent inheritance. It is here, in this unexamined middle ground, that the need for relearning first announces itself.

To truly relearn, one must first unlearn, shedding the burdens imposed by a society that measures mortal lives by immortal clocks, pressuring conformity where time's true value lies in authentic rebellion. This is the quiet tragedy: lives unbecoming, accepted without question, lost to the herd.

Join me in shattering this cycle.

> ***'Manifesto Through Encounters'***
> *"As I encounter many along my journey, I let those in,*
> *in the hope that they understand the depths of my spirit*
> *and complexity of my energy, along with the frequency*
> *that hums through my universe.*
> *A few linger, but most continue on their way.*
> *I sometimes wonder why, but pass no judgment.*
> *So, stay if you must,*
> *knowing that there are no perfect souls,*
> *only perfect intentions.*
> *Mine may be misunderstood, but are born of honor.*
> *If you take your leave, may wisdom light your journey."*

Conscious Breather

This manifesto is a meditation on the challenge of true understanding, the fleeting nature of human bonds, and the decision to honor one's intentions while offering others freedom and goodwill. It suggests a worldview rooted in acceptance, non-attachment, and the conviction that sincerity is more essential than perfection.

REFLECTIVE PAUSE: Before moving on, linger here for a moment. Think about the people who have crossed your path briefly, unexpectedly, or without explanation. Which encounters stayed with you long after they ended, and why?

Ask yourself: Who saw you more clearly than you saw yourself at the time? Who unsettled something dormant within you, even if nothing was ever said aloud? Which connections altered your direction without ever becoming part of your story?

Notice what this manifesto stirs, comfort, resistance, recognition, or quiet unease. None of it needs resolution yet. Sometimes the most meaningful shifts in a life do not arrive through permanence, but through passing presence. Contemplate that truth before continuing.

To those who stayed, those who left, and those who appeared only for a moment: your presence shifted the course of this journey in ways that may never be fully visible, but are deeply felt. This is, in part, a map of those crossings, proof that every soul who brushed against mine did so with purpose, and that nothing about our meeting was ever random.

If something in these words reaches you, let it be this: no story is ever written alone. This is, in part, your reflection too, a quiet record of the challenge you offered along the way.

For that, and for you, this work is offered with a full and grateful heart.

Preface

Here, I am truly unfiltered, and unbound. I spent decades unlearning all that inhibited my consciousness. ***Before anything here found language, it lived as tension. A quiet friction between what was expected of me and what refused to stay silent.*** This work was not born from confidence or authority, but from years of listening inward while the outer world spoke loudly about who I should be, what I should value, and how I should measure a life.

The preface that follows is not a justification for these pages, it is a threshold. A moment of pause before unlearning begins, where certainty loosens its grip and you're invited to step beyond inheritance, habit, and script, into a more deliberate relationship with thought, freedom, and self.

To that end, a seismic shift came when I penned the following:

> ***'Unlearning: The Art of Freedom'***
> *"After a lifetime of theological intoxication,*
> *I suddenly emerged and chose not to follow the flock,*
> *in defiance of the shepherd!*
> *Despite the consequences,*
> *I found myself unbranded*

and realized that I much preferred
to be in the presence of none,
than in the company of sheep!
Know, that I make no claim
as I have no right to.
I simply chose my own path
instead of the one imposed on me.
Thus, I am now free to be!"

Conscious Breather

This unlearning is an expression of breaking free from traditional constraints and seeking personal authenticity. It resonates with themes found in existential philosophy, where one seeks meaning through personal choice and responsibility. The imagery of intoxication, emergence, and solitude serves as a metaphor for the journey towards self-discovery and liberation from imposed identities.

REFLECTIVE PAUSE: Ponder with what was just said before interpreting it. Consider the beliefs you were handed before you were old enough to question them. Which ones still shape your choices, even if you no longer agree with them?

Ask yourself quietly: What ideas did you accept out of loyalty rather than understanding. Where have you followed out of habit, not conviction? If you stopped defending what you inherited, what would remain?

Unlearning rarely feels like liberation at first. It often feels like standing alone, unbranded, without shelter or script. Notice whether this piece feels

```
confronting, relieving, or disorienting. That
reaction is not accidental. Freedom does not arrive
when certainty is replaced, but when obedience ends.
```

Within the boundless tapestry of existence, where each thread carries both mystery and meaning, you are invited to walk the inward path of transformation. Through reflection and discovery, allow the silent wisdom of life to awaken within you, guiding you toward the radiant unfolding of your highest potential and the serene freedom of the soul.

Glimpses into an Unscripted Consciousness is not a title chosen for effect, but a reflection of method. It describes a living record of inner experience, thought, and awareness as they arise, unplanned and unfiltered. These pages follow consciousness in motion, before it is shaped by narrative, justification, or performance. What emerges is not a rehearsed story, but an honest encounter with perception, emotion, and reflection as they naturally unfold.

At its philosophical core, the work leans into presence and self-observation, the act of watching thought without interruption or censorship. It values spontaneity over structure, allowing insight to surface without forcing conclusion or coherence. Through this, it becomes an exercise in existential self-inquiry, documenting awareness not as a concept, but as a lived, breathing experience.

Blending memoir, philosophy, and poetic introspection, it resists linear storytelling in favor of evolution. ***It does not seek***

to explain the mind, but to witness it. The result is a portrait of consciousness learning to observe itself, rising and falling through moments of clarity, doubt, and revelation.

What is revealed are the quiet inner revolutions that occur when life is no longer lived on autopilot, when attention turns inward, and the unscripted truth is finally allowed to speak.

This is not written to agree with, but one to walk through slowly; take what resonates, question what resists, and allow what remains to meet you honestly.

Join me...

Introduction

What unfolds in these pages was never experienced in any format of a straight line. The thoughts, reflections, and encounters that shaped this work arrived scattered, overlapping, and often out of sequence. Rather than force them into artificial order, I chose to group them by resonance, allowing related ideas to find one another naturally.

To support this rhythm, each passage bearing my signature is followed by a deliberate breath, a moment of reflection, and a quiet glance forward. These pauses are not conclusions. They are invitations, spaces where one can linger, examine, and carry what was just encountered into what follows.

So, there comes a moment, quiet as a held breath, when the inner world refuses to stay in the shadows. A moment when the thoughts we tucked away, the ones we were certain were too strange or too bold or too revealing, begin to knock until the door finally swings open. This was born in that moment. Not from certainty, but from an awakening that felt raw and unplanned, like stepping into a light I did not know I had been missing.

For years, life moved along its usual tracks, shaped by inherited beliefs and the rhythm of a world that rarely pauses long enough to ask why it insists on being what it is. Then a single piece of writing, unexpected and timely, loosened everything. It questioned the faith I was raised with, the stories I trusted, and the assumptions that had quietly shaped my identity. The ground shifted. The familiar cracked. And in those cracks, I found the courage to stop performing the life I thought I was supposed to live.

What followed was a quiet rupture. Pages once scattered like forgotten feathers suddenly revealed their intent, each carrying a fragment of insight that only made sense once the floodgates opened. It dawned on me that I could step into a self I had not yet allowed to exist, one unburdened by caution or expectation. Writing through this newly formed lens, I stopped flinching. I allowed my contradictions to stand side by side. I spoke in a voice that felt unfamiliar at first, then unmistakably true.

As the years unfolded, institutions that once seemed unshakable began to crumble under the weight of their own illusions. The world revealed itself in layers, some beautiful, some brittle, all instructive. With each revelation, my writing grew sharper, more daring, more unwilling to pretend. The pieces collected in these pages were shaped in that season of unmasking, a season that asked me to let go of the scripted roles and meet my consciousness as it truly was: messy, luminous, irreverent, and awake.

This is not a map or a sermon. It is a glimpse into a mind learning to see, a record of thoughts that insisted on being written before they burned through the surface. You will find provocations here. Vulnerabilities too. Moments of clarity wrapped in questions that refuse neat endings. Every piece carries its own pulse, and every analysis attempts to trace the thread between my inner world and the collective one we share.

If there is an invitation woven through these pages, it is this: step beyond the script. Wander into the truths you have avoided. Let curiosity pry open what certainty has sealed. Consciousness is not a destination, it is an unfolding, and this is my unfolding, offered without armor.

Welcome to Glimpses into an Unscripted Consciousness.
May it stir something in you that is ready to rise.

I

The Opening Disruption

Glimpses into the what, the why, the when, the where, and the who that shaped everything that followed. It is not a straight line, nor a neatly packaged origin story.
It is a layering of moments, questions, fractures, and quiet decisions that gradually formed the foundation beneath these ideas.
Before any framework existed, before language gave structure to insight, there was lived experience, often messy, often unresolved, always instructive.
It can be provocative, intense and overpowering!

1

A Conscious Awakening

From my earliest days, a small tremor lived inside me, a whisper that something in my world sat tilted. I moved through childhood with a knot in my stomach, a soft warning that the life around me was not mine to inhabit. The streets I walked felt borrowed. The faces that surrounded me felt like strangers dressed as familiars.

Even the faith I was told to carry felt like a coat sewn for someone else's shoulders. School, society, the rituals of everyday life, all of it pressed against me until I could no longer pretend it fit. I did not belong, not in the way everyone else seemed to. And somehow, even then, I knew this unease was not a flaw in me. It was the first stirring of an awakening.

This awakening moved slowly, place to place, continent to continent, almost shyly, taking decades to gather enough courage to surface as a wish, an urge and a conviction to write. I began to spill my thoughts onto paper without any sense of where they were heading or why they insisted on arriving.

Most of what I wrote took the shape of short, cryptic lines, little fragments that spoke a private language only I could decipher. I did not care for an audience. I did not crave recognition. All I wanted was to trace the edges of the storm building inside my mind and, in the quiet act of journaling, try to understand the weather of my own soul.

Everything I wrote was simply a reflection of whatever brushed against my life that day. The smallest moments and the heavy ones all found their way onto the page, drifting across a wide landscape of themes. I had no method, no disciplined practice, no grand plan to distill meaning. I only had the urge to let my thoughts spill freely, as if getting them onto paper might help me breathe a little easier.

Over time, I gathered a strange constellation of cryptic quotes, each one a small marker on the path from who I had been to who I was becoming. Some carried the weight of an entire book, as if a single line could hold a universe. Others felt like the beginnings of a system, a quiet framework that might help someone else glimpse life differently and perhaps draw a bit of benefit from the thin strands of wisdom that rose from my restless thoughts.

And so I began, gathering my thoughts with a little more intention, giving each fragment a heading, shaping possible book titles out of the fog. When I shared a few pieces with the people I held closest, their reactions revealed something I had not considered. ***My name attached to these words would not change the reader, not in any meaningful way.*** The value lived in the message itself, not in the signature beneath it.

That realization landed heavier than I expected. It was not rejection, yet it carried the same sting, the unsettling truth that insight alone does not move people, and names do not grant ideas their power. I felt a quiet disappointment in how easily substance is divorced from source, how readily meaning is consumed without regard for the hand that shaped it. That tension became a catalyst.

Out of it came a series of sharper reflections, fragments born from disillusionment rather than ambition, each one an attempt to speak more plainly, more honestly, to see whether truth could stand on its own when stripped of ego, recognition, and reward. And so I persisted, writing with sharper clarity and deliberate intent. Much of what follows was shaped in that resolve, each piece a continuation of the same search, carried forward without compromise.

Then came the debut of Aryan Costa, a name I chose to hold the full shape of who I am, my history, my heritage, my quiet fire. Through him, I found permission to write without restraint, to wander boldly into my most provocative thoughts and open every door I had once kept locked. What had lived in the shadows began to step into the light, not as rebellion, but as a long overdue truth finally allowed to breathe.

What follows here is a glimpse into the scattered thoughts I once pressed into words, each one examined with a deeper lens to reveal the layers beneath. Together, they offer a sense of the inner terrain I had crossed, the questions that shaped me and the quiet revelations that guided my life. ***This is my conscious awakening, authentic, unfiltered, and unbound!***

2

A Global Odyssey

Greetings, I go by Aryan Costa, one, whose journey spans continents, cultures, and diverse life experiences. My nom de plume reflects my rich ethnic heritage, with ancestral roots deeply embedded on the Indian continent, while being born and raised on another, miles apart on the southern hemisphere of Africa.

During my formative years, I found myself yet on a different continent across the vast ocean, navigating a diverse and intricate world north of the Americas. This journey, which spanned thousands of miles, several time zones and a host of countries, provided me with invaluable insights into a myriad of cultures as I traveled the planet. These experiences, akin to a global odyssey, shaped my understanding of the interconnectedness of humanity.

As the pages of life turned, I found myself at a more enlightened age, once again crossing the ocean seeking a new chapter at the center of the world along the shores of southern Europe, where I now embrace all humanity has to offer. Here, I have immersed myself in the collective wisdom of many, opening my heart and mind to the universe.

This quest serves as a conduit for expanding my horizons in the realm of self-development.

As a homesick nomad, I roamed the planet in search of a space where my heart belonged. Here, I discovered inner peace, shores where I am one with the universe and the cathedral of lights, where I live my passion. Hence, my nirvana!

Constant movement carries a quiet cost that is rarely spoken about. Each relocation required a shedding of familiarity, language, rhythm, and identity, just as roots began to form. Friendships were often brief, belonging provisional, and the sense of home perpetually deferred.

I learned how to adapt quickly, how to read rooms, cultures, and unspoken rules, but that adaptability came with its own weight. Stability was something I observed in others long before I experienced it myself. There were moments of profound isolation, where motion felt less like freedom and more like drift.

Yet it was precisely this displacement that sharpened my awareness. Moving through continents stripped away assumptions I might have otherwise mistaken for truth. Each place challenged something I believed I understood, forcing reflection where certainty once lived. The absence of permanence created space for inquiry, and in that space, consciousness began to stir. What initially felt like fragmentation slowly revealed itself as preparation.

In hindsight, every crossing served a purpose. The distance I traveled externally mirrored an inner migration toward clarity. Each departure taught me what did not belong, until eventually, I recognized what did. When I finally arrived where my heart could settle, it was not by chance, but by convergence.

My words, character, journey, beliefs, and inspiration were all forged at sharp turning points of my existence and they continue to be. At a more enlightened age, I began crafting a self-definition that aligned with all aspects of who I'd become and all that framed me.

To that end, this is the legacy that defined the *Glimpses into an Unscripted Consciousness*:

> ***'Vision of Selfhood'***
>
> *"Thought provocateur, an ambivert, naturally introverted and a selectively extroverted, pronoid mystic with a nuanced moral compass.*
>
> *A vivid, imaginative, gen-x, private, authentic, unconventional, sigma male outcast, attracted only to the like-minded.*
>
> *Always grateful, somewhat mysterious, usually unapologetic and often found on the road less traveled.*
>
> *Frequently misunderstood, yet an eternal optimist.*
>
> *An agnatheist, atypical, pragmatic, spiritual and a logical free thinker with a thirst for knowledge."*

```
REFLECTIVE PAUSE: Before you continue, resist the
urge to compare. Read that self-definition again,
slowly. Not to admire it or reject it, but to notice
what it awakens in you if at all.

Ask yourself: If you were to define yourself
honestly, without audience or approval, what would
you include? Which parts of you have never made it
into language, and why? How much of who you are is
chosen, and how much was assumed over time?

Pay attention to any discomfort that arises.
Discomfort often signals proximity to truth. Most
people move through life described by others,
labeled by roles, reduced to context. Very few ever
pause long enough to name themselves deliberately.
Sit with the possibility that self-definition is not
a declaration, but a responsibility. Then continue,
carrying that question with you.
```

I remain steadfast to continue the introspection, learning and unlearning to craft a more accurate definition in time to come.

I sincerely encourage you to attempt your own definition, not as a label, but as an act of liberation. There is a quiet freedom that comes from knowing who you are, even provisionally, even imperfectly. Yet most people move through life without ever pausing to ask the question seriously.

Roles are adopted, identities are assumed, and expectations are fulfilled, but the self remains largely undefined. To name yourself, on your own terms, is to reclaim authorship. It does not fix you in place, it frees you to evolve with intention rather than drift by default.

After defining myself, gratitude replaced restlessness. Movement gave way to meaning. And the journey that once felt endless resolved itself into presence, exactly where I was meant to be.

And so, my journey continues...

3

Collective Conversion

This is where it all begins, not at the beginning, but at the moment when life started to make a strange kind of sense, or none at all. In the span of an ordinary lifetime, consider this just beyond the halfway mark, where looking back and looking forward carry equal weight.

One of the most pivotal choices of my life arrived the moment ***I read something that shook the ground beneath my long held beliefs***. It pressed me to question my faith, my assumptions and all the quiet habits we accept as the natural order of things. It was as if a single line of text reached into my life and pulled open a door I never knew was there.

> "YOU MUST ALWAYS BE WILLING TO TRULY CONSIDER EVIDENCE THAT CONTRADICTS YOUR BELIEFS, AND ADMIT THE POSSIBILITY THAT YOU MAY BE WRONG. INTELLIGENCE ISN'T KNOWING EVERYTHING. IT'S

> THE ABILITY TO CHALLENGE EVERYTHING YOU KNOW."

This passage (author, unknown) is a quiet manifesto for intellectual humility. At its core, it asks for courage rather than certainty. To consider evidence that contradicts our beliefs is not a weakness of conviction, it is a strength of character. Most people protect beliefs because those beliefs protect identity, community, and comfort. This passage invites the opposite move, to loosen the grip on being right in favor of being honest.

The second line reframes intelligence in a radical way. Intelligence is not presented as accumulation or mastery, but as elasticity. Knowing everything is static, it closes the loop. Challenging everything you know keeps the mind alive, responsive, and evolving. It recognizes that understanding is provisional, shaped by context, information, and experience, all of which change over time.

There is also an ethical undertone here. To admit the possibility of being wrong is to make room for others, for dialogue, for correction without humiliation. It dismantles arrogance without diminishing confidence. One can hold beliefs firmly while holding them lightly enough to revise when truth demands it.

Ultimately, the passage positions intelligence as an ongoing practice rather than a destination. It suggests that wisdom is not found in defending what we know, but in remaining teachable. In that sense, growth is less about replacing ignorance with knowledge and more about replacing certainty with curiosity.

These words opened a floodgate, stirring all the fragments I had gathered over the years and giving them a sudden, unexpected relevance. They cleared a path for a truth I was finally ready to admit.

That admission, quiet but seismic, became the doorway to the following quote titled:

> ***'Collective Conversion'***
> *"I was born free until society converted me.*
> *Eventually, my intellect reverted me.*
> *Thus, I now am."*

Conscious Breather

This captures a journey from innocence to awakening, from the innate freedom we are born with, to the conditioning imposed by society, and finally to the self-liberation that comes through conscious thought. It reflects the cyclical evolution of identity: freedom lost through conformity, and then reclaimed through awareness. The final phrase, "Thus, I now am," signifies not a return to the original state, but a higher form of freedom, one forged through understanding rather than ignorance.

REFLECTIVE PAUSE: Think about that for a second, pause and look outward, then inward. Consider the beliefs you share not because you chose them, but because they were everywhere. The ideas repeated so often they stopped sounding like opinions and started feeling like truth.

Ask yourself: Where did your most deeply held beliefs originate? Which of them have you examined, and which have simply followed you forward? At what point did participation begin to feel like choice?

Notice your instinctive response to the words you just read. Agreement is easy. Resistance is revealing. Collective conversion does not require force. It succeeds through repetition, comfort, and the quiet reward of belonging. Sit with the possibility that reclaiming your intellect may require standing briefly apart from the crowd. Then continue, aware of what you are carrying and why.

Forward Glance

What makes collective conversion so enduring is not force, but familiarity. Beliefs spread most efficiently when they are shared, repeated, and rarely examined. Over time, agreement replaces awareness, and participation is mistaken for choice. The danger is not that people believe, but that they stop noticing when belief becomes automatic. The moment thought is outsourced to the collective, consciousness recedes quietly, without resistance, without protest.

And that is where conversion completes its work.

4

Entitled Respect

Respect used to be earned slowly. It arrived after consistency, contribution, and quiet competence. Today, it often arrives fully formed, wrapped in filters, followers, and fleeting attention. Society has learned to applaud visibility before substance, confidence before character, and performance before proof. The louder the presence, the quicker the reverence.

Influencers and online personalities now shape opinions, habits, and values at scale, not because of demonstrated wisdom or lived credibility, but because of aesthetics, aspiration, and algorithmic reach. Glitz replaces grounding. Glamour becomes authority. A curated life is mistaken for a considered one. In this digital theater, perception outruns truth, and applause becomes evidence enough.

What makes this shift unsettling is not influence itself, but how easily respect is granted without scrutiny. We borrow beliefs from strangers we would never consult in real life. We model our lives after highlight reels, mistaking exposure for experience and popularity for insight. In doing so, respect drifts away from its original purpose, not as admiration rooted in merit, but as attention given to whoever holds the spotlight longest.

This is not an indictment of visibility, nor a rejection of modern platforms. ***It is a quiet invitation to pause and ask a harder question, what now qualifies someone as worthy of respect?*** And perhaps more importantly, who are we becoming when we stop asking for evidence before we offer it?

After watching the world long enough, noticing how it moves, who it elevates, and what it ignores, I came to see that even the most profound words from an unheralded voice rarely command instant respect.

I was no philosopher by trade, no accomplished writer with a lineage of accolades; no matter how deeply felt my insights, they would not garner the reverence of strangers simply because of the name attached or lack thereof.

Yet in that observation lies a quiet liberation: words earn their true weight not through credentials or fame, but through the raw intention and authenticity pulsing beneath them. Sometimes, it is the unknown voice, the one without pedigree or platform that people trust most instinctively, for it speaks without agenda, without the baggage of expectation.

That understanding freed me to offer these glimpses as they are, and led me to this reflection:

> ***'Entitled Respect'***
>
> *"Everyone is entitled to respect*
> *but most will never get any,*
> *and the few that do,*
> *will, for reasons not connected*
> *to the essence of the rightfully deserved respect."*

Conscious Breather

This examines the disconnect between the belief that respect is a universal right and the reality of how it is selectively distributed. It critiques a world where recognition is often granted based on status, visibility, or power rather than character or integrity. It challenges the assumption that respect naturally follows worth, revealing instead how authenticity frequently goes unnoticed while entitlement is rewarded. It ultimately invites a redefinition of respect, one grounded in essence rather than elevation.

REFLECTIVE PAUSE: Just take that in, notice where your respect goes automatically. Think about the people you admire, follow, defer to, or listen to without question. What earned that respect, presence, visibility, status, familiarity, or substance?

Ask yourself: Who do you respect before they've shown you who they are? Where have you confused confidence with credibility? Have you ever withheld respect from someone because they lacked recognition rather than merit?

Respect reveals more about the giver than the

receiver. It exposes what we value, what we fear, and what we mistake for authority. Sit with the idea that respect, when given without discernment, loses its meaning. Then move forward, aware of how, and why, you offer it.

Forward Glance

Entitlement survives by assumption, not examination. Respect, when demanded rather than earned, loses its meaning and becomes a tool of imbalance. What is freely given holds weight. What is coerced corrodes trust on both sides. The question is not who deserves respect by position or proximity, but whether respect can exist at all when it is no longer rooted in character.

Once that distinction is seen clearly, entitlement struggles to justify itself.

5

Drunk on Kool-Aid

This story lands differently. Conformity rarely announces itself as a choice. It arrives softly, dressed as belonging, acceptance, tradition, or simply "the way things are done." Most of us don't remember the moment we first agreed to it, only that one day we were already participating. The rituals felt harmless, even comforting, and questioning them seemed unnecessary, sometimes impolite. After all, everyone else was drinking from the same cup.

What makes conformity powerful is not force, but familiarity. It asks for no conviction, only compliance. Over time, repetition dulls discernment, and what once felt optional begins to feel inevitable. The cost is subtle at first, a quiet distancing from instinct, a small betrayal of preference, barely noticeable until the body or mind begins to push back.

This emerged not from rebellion, but from recognition. From realizing that what I was consuming, mentally, culturally, and ideologically, was no longer nourishing me, even if it was

widely accepted. The story that follows uses a simple metaphor to explore that realization, one that appears innocent on the surface, but carries a far broader implication beneath it.

Once again, at a more enlightened age, I set out to reconstruct something as simple as water versus Kool-Aid, and the moral woven into that choice.

> ***'Drunk on Kool-Aid'***
> *"At a tender age, I was introduced to Kool-Aid - colorful, sweet and refreshing. The alternative was water - transparent, colorless and tasteless.*
> *Admittedly, I never enjoyed Kool-Aid as much, but drank the Kool-Aid because everyone else did.*
> *Over time, I consumed less and less and eventually realized the ill-effects of this powder which was simply an unhealthy concoction diluted in water.*
> *So, I finally gave up the Kool-Aid for water - pure, natural, good for the mind, body and spirit.*
> *By advocating this shift, I realized that I was no longer in the good graces of the 'kool' crowd anymore.*
> *Just because everyone else drank the Kool-Aid doesn't mean that you have to, too.*
> *And, if you think this is about Kool-Aid, think again!"*

Conscious Breather

This is an allegory about conformity and the quiet courage required to step away from what is popular but unhealthy. Kool-Aid represents the colorful, seductive norms we consume because others do, while water symbolizes clarity, authenticity, and truth. It examines conditioning, peer pressure, and the social cost of choosing differently, ultimately affirming that true nourishment, of mind, body, and spirit, often requires walking away from the crowd.

REFLECTIVE PAUSE: Sit with that for a moment, the ideas, habits, and beliefs you accepted because they were familiar, colorful, or widely shared. Not because they nourished you, but because everyone else seemed to be drinking them.

Ask yourself: What have you continued to consume out of habit rather than alignment? Where did you silence your own taste in order to belong? What did it cost you to choose what was popular over what was clear?

Clarity is rarely celebrated. It is often labeled as difficult, boring, or disloyal. Consider where choosing what is simple and true may have quietly distanced you from the crowd.

Forward Glance

The most powerful conditioning does not announce itself as control. It presents as normal, agreeable, even comforting. By the time the taste feels familiar, questioning it feels unnecessary, sometimes disloyal. What is rarely considered is that participation does not equal consent, and repetition does not equal truth. The cup is offered daily.

Whether it is lifted again is always a choice, even when it no longer feels like one.

II

Discernment of Self

Flows naturally from 'The Opening Disruption' and marks a quiet turning inward, where wisdom matures through discernment rather than rebellion. These reflections explore authenticity, intellect, power, and the gradual refinement of thought as ego loosens its grip.

Growth here is no longer measured by victory or recognition, but by clarity, restraint, and independence of mind.

As you cross this threshold, ask yourself: where has thinking replaced reacting, and where has it not yet?

6

The Evolution of Wisdom

Wisdom begins its life as guidance. In childhood, it arrives through parents, guardians, and elders who interpret the world on our behalf. They teach us how to speak, how to behave, how to survive. At that stage, authority feels fixed. Knowledge flows in one direction, from those who know, to those who are learning.

As time moves, the balance quietly shifts. The child grows into an adult, shaped by education, exposure, and the accumulated evolution of ideas. New tools emerge, new sciences, new languages, new ways of seeing the world.

The student begins to surpass the teacher, not through disrespect, but through progress. What once felt absolute starts to feel incomplete. Wisdom evolves, not by replacing the past, but by extending beyond it.

Eventually, the roles invert. The ones who once protected us now require protection. The hands that guided begin to tremble. Memory softens, certainty fades, and consciousness itself starts to loosen its grip. ***The child becomes the guardian, not because they are wiser in every way, but because time has moved the responsibility forward.*** Wisdom, in this phase, is no longer about answers, but about patience, dignity, and care.

This cycle reveals a truth that is easy to overlook, wisdom is not owned by age, education, or authority. It migrates. It adapts. It asks to be relearned in each stage of life. And in witnessing this arc, from dependence, to independence, to interdependence, we begin to understand that wisdom is not a destination, but a responsibility passed hand to hand, until it finally returns to silence.

Along life's winding journey, we all encounter mentors, gurus, or figures we admire with awe. For our own reasons, they shape our becoming, influencing our direction, inspiring us to pursue the traits they embody.

Yet life rarely follows a straight path: those once exalted may disappoint us for reasons known or unknown, or we ourselves may evolve into the inspiration for someone we once viewed as a guide.

This turning of the tables reshapes how we regard others and how we navigate our own conduct. I took note of it and felt compelled to tell a story that probes this dynamic, giving form to my reflections. See if it resonates:

'The Evolution of Wisdom'

"In the early days of learning, a student gazes upon their teacher with wide-eyed wonder. The instructor's vast knowledge and sage advice inspires awe and deep respect in the pupil's heart.

As time unfolds, this dynamic naturally evolves as the teacher transitions into a mentor, guiding the student, now a mentee, through life's intricate pathways. Their bond strengthens, rooted in shared experiences and mutual growth.

The Turning of the Tide: *With the passage of time, the mentee's own reservoir of wisdom begins to swell. Through dedicated curiosity and life experience, they amass insights that rival, and sometimes surpass, those of their longtime guru. The flow of knowledge, once unidirectional, now becomes a two-way current.*

A Crossroads of Character: *Faced with this shift, the mentor stands at a crucial juncture, presented with two distinct paths:*

The Path of Growth: *Embrace this new dynamic with open arms. Recognize the mentee as an equal, celebrating their achievements and fostering an environment of mutual learning and shared discovery.* **Or...**

The Path of Ego: *Reject the mentee's growth, clinging to an outdated hierarchy. Allow pride and insecurity to erode the foundation of trust and respect built over years.*

The Choice That Defines Us: *The mentor's decision at this crossroads reveals the true nature of their character. Will they choose humility and continued growth, or retreat into the comfort of perceived superiority?*

> ***A Question for Reflection:*** *If you found yourself in the mentor's position, which path would you choose? How would your decision reflect your values and your vision for personal growth?*
>
> *Thus, the mentee awaits..."*

Conscious Breather

It explores how wisdom is formed not in isolation, but through relationship, time, and humility. It traces the natural progression from student to mentee to equal, revealing how true teaching succeeds only when growth is shared rather than protected. The reflection exposes the quiet test faced by those in positions of guidance: to celebrate the rise of another or to resist it in defense of ego. Ultimately, wisdom is reframed not as authority or accumulation, but as the capacity to evolve alongside others, honoring knowledge as a living exchange rather than a fixed hierarchy.

REFLECTIVE PAUSE: Let that register, think about the people who once guided you, taught you, or held authority in your life. How has your understanding of them changed over time?

Ask yourself honestly: Have you ever outgrown someone you once revered? If so, how did you respond, with humility, discomfort, gratitude, or resistance? And just as importantly, how would you respond if someone were now outgrowing you?

Wisdom is not tested when it is admired. It is tested when it is no longer needed in the same way. Notice whether this reflection places you more easily in the role of the mentee or the mentor. Both

```
positions reveal something different. Debate the
idea that true wisdom is not proven by how many
follow you, but by how freely others can walk on
without you.
```

Forward Glance

Wisdom does not announce its arrival. It reveals itself in restraint, in the willingness to release authority, and in the quiet acceptance that growth does not require hierarchy. The truest measure of wisdom is not how much one is followed, but how little one is needed once understanding takes root.

When knowledge is allowed to outgrow the one who held it, wisdom has completed its work.

7

The Authentic Self

I became aware early on that not everyone enters life through the same doors. Some arrived carrying surnames that opened rooms before a word was spoken, benefiting from reputations they did not have to earn and networks they did not have to build. Their path was eased by inheritance, by access, by familiarity with influence. Mine, unfortunately not.

Every opportunity I encountered required proof. Trust was not assumed, it was built slowly, repeatedly, and often under scrutiny. Where doors were closed, I learned to push. Where they would not move, I learned to work around them or create my own entry.

Reputation, for me, was not a byproduct of association, but the cumulative result of consistency, resilience, and accountability across every environment I stepped into.

This reality did not harden me, but it clarified something essential. When nothing is given, authenticity becomes unavoidable. ***There is no borrowed credibility to hide behind, no lineage to lean on, only the integrity of one's actions over time.*** The recognition that followed was not granted out of favor, but earned through endurance. And in that, the self that emerged was not curated, but constructed, deliberately, honestly, and entirely my own.

Identity is often inherited before it is chosen. Names, roles, expectations, and affiliations arrive early, handed down with the assumption that we will wear them faithfully.

For many, belonging is granted through association, lineage, or proximity to influence. For others, entry is quieter, earned not through invitation but through consistency, character, and time.

When nothing is given, everything is built. Reputation is not inherited, it is accumulated through conduct, resilience, and the willingness to stand exposed without guarantee of recognition. In such a life, credibility is forged slowly, across disciplines, relationships, and decisions, until presence itself becomes the introduction. You are not ushered in, you arrive carrying proof rather than permission.

This reflection emerges from that lived reality. Not as a claim of exception, but as an acknowledgment that authenticity often demands patience and perseverance. To walk one's own path is to accept that recognition, when it comes, must be earned repeatedly, in every arena of life.

> ***The Authentic Self'***
> *"You may have been ushered in by names you carry.*
> *I walked in by myself."*

Conscious Breather

It explores identity as something constructed through action rather than conferred through status. It honors the discipline of earning reputation across contexts, where recognition follows integrity instead of entitlement. It stands not as a declaration of superiority, but as evidence of a self shaped through lived accountability, presence, and the courage to arrive without borrowed credibility.

REFLECTIVE PAUSE: Pause here, without explanation. Consider how you entered the rooms that shaped your life. Which doors opened easily, and which required persistence, proof, or endurance?

Ask yourself: How much of who you are was built, rather than inherited? Where have you relied on association, and where have you stood alone? If everything external were stripped away, what would still speak for you?

Authenticity is rarely loud. It forms slowly, through consistency, accountability, and time. Notice whether this piece feels affirming or confronting. Both reactions point to something worth examining. Ponder the possibility that the most solid identity is the one that does not need to be introduced. Then continue, carrying that weight forward.

Forward Glance

Authenticity does not seek recognition, it withstands the absence of it. When reputation is built rather than inherited, identity no longer depends on access, approval, or association. What remains is a self that does not need to be announced or explained. It stands on its own history, shaped by consistency rather than circumstance.

And once that solidity is reached, authenticity becomes less about proving who you are, and more about refusing to be anything else.

8

The Unsuccessful Win

Winning has long been celebrated as proof of worth. We are taught early to measure success by comparison, by how far ahead we stand once others fall behind. Yet there are moments when victory arrives carrying an unexpected weight, a discomfort that lingers long after the outcome is decided. Not every win feels earned in spirit, even when it is earned by the rules.

There were times when achievement placed me in rooms where abundance was assumed, while others nearby carried scarcity without voice or leverage. In those moments, triumph felt hollow. ***Advancement built on imbalance revealed itself as fragile, unable to satisfy the conscience.*** To rise while others remain unseen is a form of success that quietly fails the soul.

Yet the discomfort lingered. Not as regret, but as a quiet resistance within me. It came from somewhere older than the moment itself, shaped by upbringing, cultural conditioning, and an inherited sense of right and wrong that no outcome could silence. What was celebrated externally did not sit comfortably internally. The victory asked me to ignore a part of myself I had been taught to protect.

There was guilt, but not the dramatic kind. It was subtle, almost polite. A sense that I had crossed an invisible line, not by doing something overtly wrong, but by consenting to something that felt misaligned. ***Integrity, I learned, does not always announce itself loudly.*** Sometimes it shows up as unease, as the body refusing to fully exhale even when the mind insists that everything is fine.

In that moment, I understood that success without coherence leaves a residue. A win can still fracture you if it demands silence from your values. And so the discomfort became instructive, not as punishment, but as proof that integrity survives even when it is inconvenient. It does not argue. It waits.

This reflection was shaped by that tension. By the realization that winning often requires someone else to lose, and that such outcomes, though celebrated, can fracture empathy. Progress, when isolated, breeds distance. Growth, when shared, creates continuity.

> ***'The Unsuccessful Win'***
>
> *"To win, another has to lose.*
> *Aim to achieve instead,*
> *as true success uplifts*
> *without needing to defeat."*

Conscious Breather

It challenges the conventional definition of success by confronting the moral cost of victory built on inequality. It reflects a turning point where guilt gave way to responsibility, and achievement was redefined as something that uplifts rather than diminishes others. It affirms that true success is measured not by defeating another, but by rising in ways that leave room for others to rise as well.

REFLECTIVE PAUSE: Process that for a bit here before assigning meaning. Think about the victories in your life that felt hollow once they arrived. The moments where success was undeniable, yet something in you did not celebrate.

Ask yourself: Have you ever benefited from an outcome that cost someone else quietly? Where did achievement ask you to ignore a value you were taught to protect? Did you listen to the unease, or explain it away?

Not all wins are clean. Some succeed by the rules, yet fail the conscience. Notice whether this reflection stirs guilt, clarity, or resistance. Those reactions are not weaknesses, they are signals. Consider the idea that success measured only by outcome may fracture what integrity is trying to preserve. Then continue, aware of what kind of winning you are willing to claim.

Forward Glance

Not every victory deserves to be celebrated. Some wins reveal more about imbalance than achievement, and some outcomes ask for reflection rather than applause. When success is measured only by ascent, it leaves little room for conscience. The truest reckoning comes when the question shifts from *Did I win?* to *What did this cost, and who carried it?*

Only then does success begin to mean something more enduring.

9

The Architecture of Intellect

Much of what passes for daily life is lived on autopilot. Decisions are made reflexively, habits repeated without examination, and reactions outsourced to routine. Presence of mind is rare, not because people lack intelligence, but because thinking has been replaced by momentum. Action precedes reflection, and consequence follows later, often misunderstood.

Pragmatism is frequently mistaken for reason, yet the two are not the same. What is practical in the moment is not always what is rational in the long term.

Global events offer daily evidence of this disconnect, short-term solutions applied repeatedly despite long-term damage, policies driven by convenience rather than coherence, and actions justified by necessity rather than logic. Pragmatism without reason becomes survival thinking, efficient, but blind.

If logic were allowed to lead, outcomes would change. Logic

asks uncomfortable questions, weighs consequence, and resists emotional manipulation. It slows impulse in favor of structure. The absence of logical architecture leaves thought fragmented and easily steered.

This reflection emerged from recognizing that intellect is not proven by activity, but by intention. A world guided by reason would not be perfect, but it would be more measured, more humane, and far less destructive by default.

Intellect is often mistaken for accumulation, how much one knows, how quickly one can respond, how convincingly one can argue. ***Yet knowledge without structure collapses under pressure, and intelligence without restraint becomes noise.*** What endures is not volume of thought, but how thought is organized, tested, and applied.

Over time, I came to recognize distinct layers within the mind. Reason provides awareness, the ability to pause and observe. Pragmatism brings discernment, translating understanding into function. Logic, when sharpened and disciplined, allows ideas to stand independently of emotion or bias. Together, they form a framework, not for dominance, but for coherence.

This thought emerged as a result of learning that clarity is built, not inherited. That sound thinking requires discipline, humility, and constant recalibration. The mind, like any structure, must be designed to hold weight.

> ***'The Architecture of Intellect'***
> *"Reasoning, is the presence of mind,*
> *pragmatism is the presence of brilliance*
> *& logic is the presence of genius."*

Conscious Breather

This reframes intelligence as a system rather than a trait. It distinguishes reasoning, pragmatism, and logic as complementary pillars that support clear, resilient thought. It emphasizes intellect as something cultivated through discipline and structure, where brilliance is not loud, but precise, stable, and capable of withstanding complexity.

REFLECTIVE PAUSE: Stop, let that marinate and observe your own thinking. Notice how often your thoughts arrive fully formed, inherited, reactive, or rehearsed. How rarely they are examined for structure, coherence, or consequence.

Ask yourself: When was the last time you slowed a reaction long enough to question it. Do your beliefs rest on reasoning, pragmatism, or habit? Which parts of your thinking are disciplined, and which are simply repeated?

Intellect is not revealed by how quickly you respond, but by how carefully your thoughts are built. Consider the idea that clarity requires design. That without structure, even intelligence becomes easy to steer. Before continuing, consider whether your mind is something you inhabit, or something you have intentionally constructed.

Forward Glance

A mind without structure is easily moved, persuaded by urgency, repetition, or convenience. Presence of thought is what separates reaction from reason. Pragmatism may keep systems running, but logic is what prevents them from collapsing. When intellect is built deliberately, layered with awareness, discipline, and restraint, it becomes resistant to noise and manipulation.

In a world driven by impulse, the most radical act remains thinking clearly, on purpose.

10

When Thought Meets Power

Most thoughts are not born from reflection. They are assembled in transit. Shaped by alarms, commutes, obligations, interruptions, and the steady pressure of getting through the day. Thought, for most people, is not a deliberate act, but a by-product of survival. We think in fragments between tasks, not in stretches deep enough to challenge what we believe.

By the time the day loosens its grip, energy is spent. Intellect, which requires space and stillness, arrives too late to influence the narrative. Fatigue takes over, and whatever ideas have settled unexamined are accepted as truth. Night closes the loop, not with insight, but with exhaustion. The mind powers down without having been consulted.

Morning then resumes on autopilot. The same assumptions re-enter the system unchallenged, reinforced by repetition rather than reason. ***In this cycle, thought becomes habit, habit becomes belief, and belief becomes something we defend***

without remembering how it was formed. It is here, in this quiet erosion of awareness, that power finds its entry point.

Freedom of thought is often celebrated as an abstract right, while power is pursued as an external force. Rarely are the two examined together. Yet the moment intellect gains influence, when ideas begin to shape outcomes, decisions, or lives beyond the self, thought is no longer harmless. It carries consequence.

There comes a point where thinking clearly is not enough. ***The possession of intellect confers responsibility, not authority.*** Power without reflection becomes coercive. Thought without restraint becomes dangerous.

This reflection was born from recognizing that the most damaging acts are often committed not through ignorance, but through unexamined certainty. To think freely is a privilege. To wield that thinking in ways that affect others is a duty. Wisdom lies not in the reach of one's ideas, but in the care with which they are applied.

> ***'When Thought Meets Power'***
> *"We possess both, freedom and power.*
> *The freedom of thought and the power of intellect.*
> *Use both wisely."*

Conscious Breather

Here, we explore the intersection of intellect and responsibility. It warns against the unchecked influence of ideas divorced from ethical awareness, and reframes power as something that demands restraint rather than dominance. It affirms that true wisdom lies in using both freedom of thought and strength of intellect with humility, intention, and respect for consequence.

REFLECTIVE PAUSE: Take a moment to absorb that. Consider the influence your thoughts already have, not someday, not hypothetically, but now. In your words, your decisions, your silence, and the moments you choose not to intervene.

Ask yourself: Where does your thinking affect others beyond yourself? Have you ever mistaken being right for being responsible? When your ideas carried weight, did you pause to consider their impact, or only their accuracy?

Power does not always announce itself as authority. Sometimes it appears quietly, through influence, credibility, or timing. Notice whether this piece feels distant or personal. That distinction matters. Consider the idea that freedom of thought is not the end of accountability, but the beginning of it. Then continue, aware that intellect, once it reaches others, is never neutral.

Forward Glance

Power does not magnify wisdom by default, it magnifies whatever thought it adopts. When reflection is absent, influence accelerates error rather than insight. The greater the reach, the heavier the obligation to question oneself before acting on others. Thought that refuses scrutiny becomes dangerous the moment it gains authority.

And power, once granted, rarely corrects what thinking failed to examine.

III

The Artist Inside

After the careful "Discernment of Self' this is devoted to deliberate reinvention, the recalibration of self through honesty and intent.
These reflections examine transformation, boundaries, self-acceptance, and the discipline of redirecting focus.
Growth here is no longer reactive, but intentional, shaped by energy matched wisely and truths owned fully.
As you approach, consider where change has been resisted, and where becoming unrecognizable may be the truest form of progress.

11

The Art of Reinvention

How many of us are willing to admit we might be broken? And even if we do, how do we discern which parts need mending, or reorganize our inner core to face life's challenges anew?

Most of us accept ourselves by default. We inherit an identity early, shaped by family, culture, expectation, and circumstance, and then spend years assuming that this must be who we are meant to be. The label sticks, not because it was chosen, but because it was never questioned. Over time, familiarity masquerades as truth.

The daily grind reinforces this acceptance. Attention is spent outward, on tasks, roles, and responsibilities, leaving little room for internal inquiry. We move from obligation to obligation, measuring our days by completion rather than consideration. In that rhythm, there is no space, and often no permission, to ask what feels aligned, what feels imposed, or what has quietly outgrown us.

What is, becomes mistaken for what should be, simply because it has gone unexamined.

At the supposed three-quarters mark of existence, I took a long, unflinching look within, confronting what lay out of alignment. ***I resolved on a monumental shift in attitude and behavior, regardless of the consequences for it was time for change, a transformation so profound it would reshape my very essence and leave me unrecognizable to my former self at which point my pen described what I intended.***

There comes a moment when survival turns into authorship. When the fractures stop being something to hide and become something to work with. This quote is spoken from that moment. It is not an apology for change, nor a defense of distance. It is a quiet truth offered to anyone who wonders why familiarity no longer fits.

> ***'The Art of Reinvention'***
> *"If you don't recognize me,*
> *it's because I put back*
> *the broken pieces*
> *together differently."*

Conscious Breather

What you are seeing is not disappearance, but deliberate rearrangement. The same pieces exist, touched by experience, placed with intention, aligned with a deeper understanding of self. The words speak to transformation through resilience and choice. It acknowledges that being broken is not the end of identity, but the beginning of reconstruction.

Rather than returning to a previous version of self, it honors the act of rebuilding with new awareness, values, and strength. Any sense of unfamiliarity others may feel is not a loss, but evidence of growth.

Often, it is those closest to you who feel this shift most sharply. Familiar patterns change, old access points close, and the version of you they once knew no longer responds in the same way. To them, this can look like distance, rebellion, or detachment. Not because you have hardened, but because you have learned where to place your energy.

Growth quietly redraws boundaries, and when closeness was built on who you used to be, it can feel like loss to those who have not yet met who you are becoming. At its heart, the message affirms personal autonomy, the courage to evolve, and the beauty found in becoming someone truer than before.

REFLECTIVE PAUSE: Let it settle in and hold here without rushing to justify anything. Think about the versions of yourself that no longer fit. The roles, behaviors, or identities you kept alive long after they stopped serving you.

Ask yourself: What parts of you have been rearranged rather than repaired? Who struggled most when you changed, you or those who expected you to stay the same? If you are no longer recognizable to some, what does that say about how far you've come?

```
Reinvention is rarely understood from the outside.
It often looks like distance to those who benefited
from your former shape. Notice whether this
reflection brings grief, relief, or resolve. Each
reaction carries information. Sit with the idea that
becoming unrecognizable can be an act of integrity
rather than escape. Then continue, knowing that
reinvention is not erasure, it is authorship.
```

Forward Glance

Reinvention is not an escape from who you were, but an honest response to who you have become. It asks for courage without spectacle, change without apology, and movement without permission. What matters is not how often you reinvent yourself, but whether each version is closer to truth than the last. When reinvention is chosen consciously, it stops being a reaction to loss and becomes an expression of agency.

And from that place, becoming is no longer accidental, it is deliberate.

12

The Art of Matching Energy

No relationship is perfectly aligned. Yet most of us behave as though it should be, or worse, as though it already is. We enter connections assuming balance exists by default, without pausing to reflect on who we are bringing into the space, or what the other person is carrying with them. Alignment is presumed, not examined.

In the absence of reflection, mismatches go unnoticed. We respond from habit rather than intention, offering energy without considering whether it is compatible, appropriate, or even welcome.

We mirror roles we have learned elsewhere, not the reality in front of us. In doing so, we miss the subtle work required to create balance, the adjustment of pace, tone, and presence that healthy relationships quietly demand.

This is where friction is born. Not from malice, but from assumption. From the belief that connection should feel effortless, when in truth, it asks for attention. ***Matching energy is not about equal output, but conscious exchange.*** And that awareness begins only when we stop assuming and start observing.

The paradox of expectation and reciprocity is as old as human connection itself, yet we still treat it as an unspoken contract. The moment one sees it for what it is, not truly mutual, not even close, a new clarity emerges: there must be another way.

Human connection is often governed by unspoken expectations. ***We speak of unconditional love and unconditional respect as ideals, yet quietly recoil when they are not returned in kind.*** In practice, these absolutes collapse under the weight of human limitation, leaving behind resentment where honesty should have lived.

This reflection emerged from releasing the pursuit of perfection in relationships. From recognizing that giving endlessly to those who do not reciprocate is not generosity, but self-erasure.

Matching energy is not transaction, it is calibration. It is the discipline of meeting others where they actually stand, not where we wish they would be.

To mirror is not to manipulate, but to remain aligned. It is a way of preserving balance without performance, of honoring both self and other without illusion.

And indeed there is, as this reveals…

> ***'The Art of Matching Energy'***
> *"I seek unconditional respect.*
> *You, unconditional love.*
> *Both, unattainable ideals.*
> *Mutual respect and love?*
> *A mere illusion.*
> *Instead, I'll mirror your feelings*
> *with my own."*

Conscious Breather

This dismantles the myth of unconditional exchange in human relationships. It reframes connection as a dynamic balance rooted in awareness and reciprocity rather than idealized expectation. It affirms matching energy as an act of self-respect, emotional intelligence, and ethical clarity, where authenticity replaces overextension and equilibrium replaces sacrifice.

REFLECTIVE PAUSE: Soak that up and take a moment before moving on, take a breath and notice how you give. Think about the relationships where your effort outweighed the return. Not out of generosity, but out of hope, habit, or fear of withdrawal.

Reflect on this honestly: Where have you offered more than was met? When did generosity quietly become self-erasure? What changed the moment you stopped matching intention and started matching energy?

Matching energy is not about withholding, it's about accuracy. It reveals what is actually present, not

```
what we wish were there. Bear in mind that balance
is not created through sacrifice alone. Sometimes
clarity arrives the moment you adjust your output to
reality. Then continue, aware that alignment begins
when effort is no longer automatic, but intentional.
```

Forward Glance

Matching energy is not withdrawal, it is calibration. It allows generosity without depletion and connection without self-erasure. When effort is aligned rather than forced, resentment has no place to grow. The discipline lies not in giving more, but in giving honestly.

And once energy is matched with intention, relationships reveal themselves clearly, without confusion, without performance, and without debt.

13

The Art of Self Acceptance

Nobody likes to fail. More accurately, nobody likes to admit that they have. Failure bruises the image we hold of ourselves, so we learn to soften it, rename it, or push it outward. We justify our actions, rationalize outcomes, or assign blame, even when the misstep is clearly our own. In doing so, we protect the ego, but delay understanding.

What often goes unacknowledged is that this avoidance is not dishonesty, it is discomfort. To sit with failure requires stillness and humility, two things rarely encouraged in a world that prizes momentum and appearances. ***It feels safer to explain ourselves away than to confront the gap between intention and result.*** Yet every justification becomes a quiet refusal to see ourselves clearly.

Self-acceptance begins where explanation ends. Not in excusing what happened, but in owning it without collapse or defense. Until we allow failure to exist without distortion, we cannot meet ourselves honestly. And without honesty, acceptance remains a performance rather than a practice. It is often misunderstood as approval, as though acknowledging oneself requires overlooking failure or dismissing responsibility. In truth, it begins where illusion ends. It is the quiet act of standing honestly with who you are, without apology and without denial.

There were many moments where the world's measurements failed to reflect my own. ***Judged by standards that rewarded conformity over character, I learned early that worth is not always recognized where it exists.*** What remained consistent, even in failure, was loyalty to my values, integrity in my conduct, and an unwillingness to abandon myself for approval.

This reflection was shaped by that realization. That acceptance is not granted by consensus, but earned through alignment. To accept oneself is not to claim perfection, but to refuse self-betrayal.

> ***'The Art of Self Acceptance'***
> *"I may have failed at much, but I have yet to fail you and most of all, me!*
> *Society judges with a unit of measure based on another's standard.*
> *Some, instead embrace my loyalty, authenticity, integrity and all that I am."*

Conscious Breather

It reframes acceptance as an act of integrity rather than

indulgence. It acknowledges failure without surrendering self-worth, and rejects external judgment as the final arbiter of value. It also affirms self-acceptance as the courage to remain loyal to oneself, even when recognition, validation, or understanding is withheld.

```
REFLECTIVE PAUSE: Give that a moment to land, slow
down and turn inward. Think about the moments you
judged yourself most harshly. Not because you
failed, but because you didn't meet a standard that
wasn't truly yours.

Reflect on this: Where have you confused
accountability with punishment? Which parts of
yourself have you accepted only conditionally? What
would it look like to acknowledge failure without
withdrawing self-respect?

Self-acceptance is not resignation. It is the
refusal to abandon yourself while learning. Bear in
mind that growth does not require self-denial to be
real. Sometimes it begins the moment honesty
replaces self-judgment. Then continue, knowing that
acceptance is not the end of becoming, but the
ground it stands on.
```

Forward Glance

Self-acceptance is not approval of everything we are, but honesty about what we carry. It does not erase failure, it places it in context. When judgment loses its grip, growth no longer requires punishment to proceed. Acceptance becomes the ground from which change can occur without violence toward the self. ***And from that ground, integrity remains intact, regardless of who is watching or who never will.***

14

The Art of Shifting Focus

Anxiety, depression, burnout, and emotional exhaustion are no longer exceptions, they are common conditions of a mental health crisis. Beneath much of this suffering lies unresolved trauma, both inherited and lived, experiences that remain active in the nervous system long after the events themselves have passed.

Trauma has a way of anchoring attention to the past or projecting it endlessly into the future. When the mind is trapped in replay or anticipation, presence becomes inaccessible. Many are not failing to focus, they are protecting themselves from pain by staying vigilant. The cost of that vigilance is exhaustion.

This contemplation was inspired from recognizing that healing does not always require revisiting every wound. Sometimes recovery begins with redirecting attention toward safety, growth, and what is still possible. ***Shifting focus is not denial of trauma, it is a conscious decision to stop allowing it to***

dominate the present. In a world carrying so much unresolved pain, reclaiming attention becomes an act of survival and self-compassion.

For a long time, I believed that revisiting pain was a form of understanding it. That if I returned to certain moments often enough, I might finally extract meaning, closure, or relief. Instead, I learned that repetition does not heal, it deepens the imprint. What began as memory slowly turned into weight.

There were chapters of my life I kept reopening, not because they still held lessons, but because they had become familiar. Trauma has a way of disguising itself as unfinished business, convincing us that staying close to it is an act of courage. In truth, it was costing me presence, clarity, and forward motion.

This thought emerged as a result of the moment I chose to redirect my attention, not away from responsibility, but away from rumination. Shifting focus was not avoidance, it was preservation. It was the decision to stop feeding what hurt me and begin investing in what could still grow.

> ***'The Art of Shifting Focus'***
> *"Trauma transforms into pain*
> *when constantly revisited.*
> *Left unchecked, it will deepen*
> *until you shift your focus elsewhere."*

Conscious Breather

This explores the personal discipline of redirecting attention away from persistent pain and toward healing. It reframes focus as an active choice, where trauma loses its grip not through denial, but through conscious disengagement. It also affirms that growth begins when attention is reclaimed and directed toward what restores rather than reopens.

REFLECTIVE PAUSE: Step back, take a moment, think about that for a second and notice where your attention rests most often. Think about the memories, worries, or scenarios you return to repeatedly. Not because they help you, but because they are familiar.

Reflect on this gently: What do you revisit that no longer teaches you anything new? Where has reflection turned into rumination? What might change if attention were redirected rather than explained?

Focus is not denial. It is selection. Healing does not always come from revisiting what hurt. Sometimes it begins when you stop feeding it. Be aware that attention is a choice, and where it rests quietly shapes what grows.

Forward Glance

Attention is one of the few resources we still underestimate. Where it rests determines what is reinforced, repeated, and eventually believed. Trauma pulls focus backward, fear pushes it forward, and both steal presence from the only place where healing can occur. Shifting focus is not forgetting, it is choosing where life is allowed to continue. ***And in that choice, the mind begins to recover its capacity to rest.***

15

The Quiet Art of Repositioning

It is human nature to test boundaries, sometimes out of curiosity, sometimes out of need, and sometimes without awareness at all. Most crossings are not malicious. They happen in moments of closeness, familiarity, or assumption. Yet there is a more subtle truth that reveals itself over time.

Those who understand boundaries best are often the ones most willing to ignore them when it suits them. Familiarity breeds entitlement. Access becomes expectation. Understanding becomes leverage. ***When someone knows where the line is, crossing it can feel intentional rather than accidental, justified by history, proximity, or perceived importance.*** What is framed as closeness quietly becomes intrusion.

We are required to recognise that boundaries are not violated because they are unclear, but because they are inconvenient. Repositioning, then, is not a reaction to ignorance, but a response to repeated choice. It is the quiet assertion that awareness does not grant permission, and that respect is proven not by knowing the boundary, but by honoring it consistently.

Some lines are noticed only after they are crossed, and some crossings are not misunderstandings, but choices. There came a point where repeating myself felt like self-neglect. Where proximity became permission, and patience was mistaken for tolerance. Repositioning did not arrive as confrontation, but as distance. Not withdrawal, but recalibration. A subtle shift that required no announcement, only resolve.

This reflection was born from learning that peace is often protected quietly. That moving a boundary far enough prevents the need to defend it again. Not everyone deserves continued access, and not every explanation is owed.

> ***The Quiet Art of Repositioning'***
> *"For one's own sanity,*
> *when another crosses a boundary,*
> *be sure to reposition the boundary far enough*
> *that they never come close to it ever again."*

Conscious Breather

Here we explore boundary-setting as a deliberate, understated act of self-preservation. It reframes distance not as punishment, but as clarity, and repositioning as a mature response to repeated transgression. It also affirms that the strongest boundaries are often the least dramatic, enforced through consistency, not confrontation.

REFLECTIVE PAUSE: Let that hit different. Think about the boundaries you explained repeatedly, hoping clarity would be enough. The lines that were understood, yet crossed anyway.

Reflect on this honestly: Where did patience begin to resemble permission? Who benefited most from your willingness to explain again? At what point did silence become the clearest response?

Repositioning is not punishment. It is recalibration. Bear in mind that not all boundaries are meant to be defended out loud. Some are preserved only by distance. Then continue, knowing that peace is often protected not by confrontation, but by where you choose to stand.

Forward Glance

Repositioning is rarely loud because it does not seek recognition. It occurs when understanding replaces explanation and distance replaces debate. Boundaries are crossed not only through ignorance, but through entitlement, and clarity often arrives only after patterns repeat. The quiet shift is not punishment, it is preservation.

And once repositioned, peace no longer needs to be defended, it simply remains.

IV

The Reckoning Phase

Knowing 'The Artist Inside', now let's confront the reckoning that follows awareness.
It explores second discoveries, gratitude earned through loss, freedom chosen through consequence and, compassion held without surrender.
Desire is questioned, expectation dismantled and, maturity forged through restraint.
Growth here is no longer idealistic, but grounded in sober self-honesty.
Stepping in, ask yourself what clarity has already cost you, and what it is still asking you to release?

16

The Second Discovery

There is a first knowing we form of people, the one built on what they choose to show and what we are willing to see. It feels sufficient at the time. Comfortable, even. I learned that the second discovery arrives only when closeness deepens and certainty dissolves.

The second discovery was more personal. I came to understand that even those closest to us, the ones we trust, love, and assume we know, only truly reveal themselves once we consciously remove the blinkers we wear. Those blinders are not ignorance, but hope, loyalty, and the desire for harmony. They can take years, sometimes a lifetime, to loosen. We often mistake familiarity for truth, and proximity for understanding.

What mattered most was realizing that it is never too late to see clearly. Awareness does not invalidate the past, nor does it erase affection, but it does ask for honesty. ***Once the veil lifts, something must change, whether that change is a boundary, a distance, or a recalibration of expectation.*** Choosing to act on that clarity is not betrayal, it is self-preservation. And sometimes, well being begins not with discovery itself, but with the courage to respond to what has been revealed.

I have met people who seemed familiar until proximity revealed what distance had concealed. The risk was never in not knowing, but in realizing too late that knowing more changes everything. Truth, once uncovered, cannot be unseen, and intimacy carries the quiet danger of disillusionment.

This reflection was shaped by those moments. By understanding that deeper knowledge is not always comforting, but it is always clarifying. To truly know someone is to accept that discovery comes with consequence.

> ***'The Second Discovery'***
> *"You really don't know a person*
> *until you get to know a person,*
> *the risk after, is knowing*
> *what you didn't know before."*

Conscious Breather

This examines the shift that occurs when surface understanding gives way to deeper truth. It reflects on the risk inherent in intimacy, where knowledge can both connect and unsettle. It also affirms that true understanding often arrives at a cost, but that clarity, however uncomfortable, is preferable to illusion.

```
REFLECTIVE PAUSE:  Just take that in, reflect on
what was revealed. Think about the people you
believed you understood, until proximity changed the
picture. The moment familiarity gave way to clarity.

Reflect on this carefully: What did you learn only
after the blinders came off? How long did you sense
the truth before you allowed yourself to see it?
What changed once you could no longer unknow it?

Second discoveries are rarely gentle. They don't
erase affection, but they do demand honesty. Hold
this awareness without rushing to judge it. Some
truths are not meant to comfort, only to clarify.
Carry this forward as you continue, knowing that
seeing clearly often costs more than not seeing at
all.
```

Forward Glance

The first understanding is built on hope, projection, and what we are willing to believe. The second arrives without ceremony, often after closeness has removed illusion. What is revealed cannot be unseen, and pretending otherwise only prolongs confusion. Discovery does not always bring comfort, but it does bring coherence.

And once coherence is present, continuing without it becomes the greater risk.

17

Gratitude After the Fall

How often do we take for granted what has been gifted to us. Not only the visible, worldly possessions that are easy to measure, but the quieter allowances that make life livable, health, stability, opportunity, time, and the unseen support that holds it all together. These are rarely earned in full, yet quickly assumed as permanent. We live inside conditions many would envy, without ever pausing to name them as such.

In that absence of gratitude, something subtle begins to shift. What exists starts to feel guaranteed. What is present feels ordinary. ***Appreciation gives way to expectation, and expectation slowly erodes care. It is not punishment that follows, but consequence.*** When gratitude fades, so does attentiveness, and what is no longer noticed becomes vulnerable to loss.

Only after the fall do many of us recognize what was carrying us. Not because it suddenly became valuable, but because it is no longer there. Gratitude, then, is not a reaction to abundance, but a discipline born of awareness. And sometimes, it takes the breaking of what was assumed to remind us of the quiet miracle it once was.

I did not learn gratitude while things were intact. It arrived later, after loss had stripped away what I once assumed was permanent. What remained was not bitterness, but a sobering clarity about how easily appreciation is postponed when comfort feels guaranteed.

There were moments I overlooked what was present because it was familiar. Security dulls awareness, and abundance often goes unnoticed until it withdraws. The fall was not dramatic, but it was decisive. It forced me to see what I had taken for granted, and to measure value more honestly.

This insight stemmed from that reckoning. Gratitude did not appear as virtue, but as consequence. Loss became the teacher that presence had failed to be.

> ***'Gratitude After the Fall'***
> *"Each selfish act of un-appreciation*
> *for what we have,*
> *will lead to an unselfish act*
> *of appreciation once it's lost."*

Conscious Breather

This explores how appreciation often follows deprivation rather than abundance. It reflects on loss as a catalyst for awareness, revealing how entitlement erodes gratitude until absence restores perspective. It also affirms gratitude not as optimism, but as earned clarity shaped by experience.

REFLECTIVE PAUSE: Slow down and look at what is still standing. Think about the things in your life that once felt guaranteed. The supports you rarely named because they were simply there.

Reflect on this honestly: What did you appreciate only after it was gone? Where did comfort quietly turn into expectation? If nothing changed tomorrow, what would you finally acknowledge today?

Gratitude does not always arrive through abundance. Often, it arrives through absence. Let this register without regret. Clarity earned through loss does not need to be softened. Move ahead with this awareness, knowing that what we notice before it breaks rarely needs to teach us the hard way.

Forward Glance

Gratitude that arrives before loss is often theoretical. Gratitude that arrives after it is informed. When what once felt permanent is removed, appreciation sharpens and illusion dissolves. The fall does not make one grateful by force, it makes gratitude unavoidable by contrast.

What remains is not optimism, but clarity, a recognition of what truly mattered, revealed only once it was no longer guaranteed.

18

The Economics of Freedom

Freedom is often spoken of as a right, but rarely as a practice. We are born with the ability to choose, yet we exercise that ability far less than we assume. Most decisions are not made deliberately, they are inherited, deferred, or quietly accepted. Choice exists, but remains largely unspent.

Over time, unrealized choices harden into routine. What began as a decision becomes a default, and eventually, a norm of day-to-day life. ***We follow patterns not because they are the only options, but because they are familiar.***

In this rhythm, the question of choice stops appearing altogether. We no longer ask whether we could act differently, only whether we should keep up.

This is how freedom is slowly outsourced. Not taken, but neglected. When every path feels preselected, responsibility fades, and with it, the awareness that even in constraint, a choice still exists. The economics of freedom begin here, not in what is denied to us, but in what we fail to claim.

Freedom is often spoken of as a right, but rarely examined as a choice with cost. ***I learned that every form of freedom demands payment, not always in money, but in comfort, security, approval, or certainty.*** What we call independence is often simply a willingness to accept those costs without complaint.

There were paths that promised stability if I agreed to trade autonomy for predictability. The exchange was tempting. Safety is seductive when it asks only for silence or compliance. Yet each compromise carried a quiet tax, one paid in restlessness, resentment, or the slow erosion of self-respect.

This reflection emerged from recognizing that quality of life is dictated not by what we possess, but by what we refuse to surrender. Freedom is not free, but it is precise. It rewards those who understand its pricing and are willing to budget accordingly.

> ***'The Economics of Freedom'***
> *"Quality of life is dictated by the freedoms one chooses."*

Conscious Breather

It reframes freedom as an intentional investment rather than an abstract ideal. It explores the hidden costs of security, conformity, and comfort, and contrasts them with the deliberate sacrifices required for autonomy. It also affirms that true freedom is measured not by abundance, but by alignment, and that every life reflects the choices one is willing to pay for.

REFLECTIVE PAUSE: Let that register, look at the real costs you carry. Think about the freedoms you desire, not in theory, but in practice. The ones that require trade-offs you rarely see advertised.

Reflect on this with honesty: What has your freedom already cost you? Which comforts did you exchange, knowingly or not, for independence? Are you paying with time, security, approval, or peace?

Freedom is never free. It is financed by choice, and sustained by consequence. Take this into account without resentment. Every life pays something, the question is whether the expense is chosen or inherited. Step forward with this in mind, aware that freedom gains value when its price is understood.

Forward Glance

Freedom is never granted without cost, only disguised. Comfort, approval, and security each carry their own price, and someone always pays it. The difference lies in who consents to the exchange. When freedom is understood as an investment rather than an entitlement, its value becomes clear.

What limits most lives is not lack of opportunity, but the unwillingness to accept the price autonomy demands.

19

Compassion Without Compromise

We tolerate far more than we should. Not because we agree with what is being done to us, but because of what we fear losing if we speak. Relationships carry weight, history, dependence, familiarity, and the unspoken threat of absence. In that dynamic, wrongdoing is often endured quietly, reframed as patience, loyalty, or understanding.

Speaking up rarely feels safe. The cost appears immediate and personal, while the benefit feels uncertain and distant. To challenge behavior risks conflict, distance, rejection, or collapse of the relationship itself. So silence becomes the compromise, and endurance is mistaken for virtue. What begins as compassion slowly hardens into permission.

Yet compassion without boundaries is not kindness, it is self-neglect. Accepting harm as a norm does not preserve connection, it distorts it. ***True compassion does not require surrendering dignity. It asks for clarity, not cruelty.***

And sometimes, the most compassionate act is not endurance, but refusal.

Compassion does not require submission. I learned that caring deeply and tolerating harm are not the same act, even though they are often confused. For a long time, I believed that understanding another's wounds obligated me to endure their behavior. Experience corrected that belief.

There came a point where forgiveness had to end where repetition began. To excuse patterns under the banner of empathy was not kindness, it was neglect of self. ***Standing firm was not a loss of compassion, but its refinement.*** It was the recognition that boundaries are not punishments, they are conditions for continued access.

This contemplation was inspired by choosing clarity over guilt. From refusing to allow empathy to be weaponized against my own well-being.

> ***'Compassion Without Compromise'***
> *"Forgive once but refuse to tolerate misgivings twice."*

Conscious Breather

This asserts that empathy does not require self-sacrifice. It draws a clear line between forgiveness and tolerance, affirming that compassion can coexist with firm boundaries. It also upholds accountability as an extension of care, where kindness remains intact without surrendering self-respect.

REFLECTIVE PAUSE: Process that for a bit, ponder before responding. Think about the times you extended understanding while quietly abandoning your own limits. The moments where kindness blurred into self-betrayal.

Reflect on this carefully: Where did compassion cost you clarity? Who benefited when you chose empathy over honesty? What would it look like to remain humane without yielding ground?

Compassion does not require collapse. It asks for presence, not permission. Let this remain present without defensiveness. Strength and care are not opposites, they are partners. Move ahead with this awareness, knowing that boundaries do not erase empathy, they protect it.

Forward Glance

Compassion loses its meaning when it requires self-erasure. To care does not obligate endurance of harm, nor does understanding excuse repetition. Boundaries do not negate empathy, they preserve it. When compassion is guided by clarity rather than guilt, it remains intact without becoming a liability.

And in that balance, care is no longer a weakness, but a strength that knows its limits.

20

When Desire Turns to Discontent

We often confuse expectation with assumption. What we believe to be a neutral framing of what is, is usually a quiet demand of what should be. Assumptions feel passive, almost innocent.

Expectations, by contrast, carry weight. They ask something of the world, of others, of outcomes. Yet we disguise the latter as the former, and in doing so, avoid responsibility for the pressure we place.

We do this everywhere and with everyone. We assume people will act a certain way, situations will unfold predictably, effort will be met with return. Because these assumptions are unspoken, they feel reasonable, even invisible. They live beneath awareness, shaping desire without ever declaring themselves.

By the time we realize that an assumption was, in truth, an expectation, it is already too late. Disappointment has settled in. Desire has turned brittle.

What could have been curiosity becomes resentment, not because reality failed us, but because it refused to obey a rule it never agreed to. And it is here, in this quiet miscalculation, that discontent takes root.

Desire was never fleeting for me, it was persistent. Each time I believed I had clarified what I wanted, expectation quietly followed. And with expectation came the subtle erosion of contentment. What began as longing gradually transformed into dissatisfaction, not because the desire was wrong, but because it demanded an outcome.

I watched this pattern repeat across relationships, pursuits, and ambitions. The moment wanting hardened into needing, peace thinned. Fulfillment became conditional, dependent on something external arriving, changing, or remaining. Desire, once innocent, began to negotiate terms it could not guarantee.

This reflection emerged from living that loop often enough to recognize it. Discontent was not a failure of desire, but a signal that expectation had taken the wheel.

> ***'When Desire Turns to Discontent'***
> *"Any form of expectation will usually lead to some level of disappointment."*

Conscious Breather

This examines the recurring tension between wanting and

fulfillment. It reflects on how desire, when tethered to expectation, quietly undermines contentment. It also affirms awareness as the interruption point, where desire can exist without demanding satisfaction, and peace is reclaimed through release rather than attainment.

REFLECTIVE PAUSE: Take a breather, slow down and look at what you've been reaching for. Think about the desires that once energized you, then gradually began to drain you. The wants that promised fulfillment but delivered restlessness instead.

Reflect on this without judgment: What did you believe this desire would fix? When did wanting more start to feel like needing less? Were you chasing growth, or avoiding stillness?

Desire is not the problem. Unexamined desire is. Let this register quietly. Discontent often signals misalignment, not failure. Carry this forward as you move on, aware that fulfillment rarely comes from accumulation, but from discernment.

Forward Glance

Desire becomes corrosive the moment it demands fulfillment as proof of worth or peace. What once inspired movement begins to generate dissatisfaction, not because wanting is wrong, but because expectation tightens its grip. Contentment does not disappear through lack, it erodes through insistence. When desire is observed without attachment, it regains its innocence.

And in that awareness, discontent loses its authority.

V

Quiet Authority

Following 'The Reckoning Phase', it's time to explore the unseen forces that shape conduct, influence and inner authority.

These reflections examine guidance given and withdrawn, the weight of silence, the discipline of response, and power that never announces itself.

Wisdom here is revealed not in control or noise, but in restraint, awareness, and clarity of thought.

Upon entering, consider where influence has been exercised quietly, and where silence has carried more authority than action.

21

The Legacy of Guidance

History is filled with recognized leaders, across time, culture, and distance. Figures of power, vision, and authority who shaped nations, movements, and belief systems. Yet when we look closer, a quieter question emerges, how many of them chose to step aside consciously, empowering the next wave to continue where they left off?

Whether heads of state, royalty, religious leaders, or cultural figureheads, the pattern repeats itself. Power is rarely released willingly. Instead of transitioning with intention, many remain until erosion takes over. Wisdom dulls, adaptability fades, and relevance thins, yet position is clung to. Authority lingers long after clarity has begun to slip.

What is most striking is not the inevitability of decline, but the resistance to departure. Leadership often ends not through foresight, but through collapse, removal, or death. Guidance is withheld until no alternative remains. In doing so, legacy narrows. What could have been continuity becomes interruption, and what might have been empowerment becomes absence. ***The true legacy of guidance is not how long one leads, but how well one prepares others to lead without them.***

Every leadership role I held came with an unspoken temptation, to stay longer than necessary, to remain central, to confuse usefulness with indispensability. Early on, I learned that guidance is most effective when it prepares others to move without you. Anything else is not leadership, it is dependency dressed as direction.

I have stood at the front long enough to know when presence empowers and when it inhibits. The measure was never how closely people followed, but how confidently they continued once space was created. True guidance required restraint, knowing when to step forward, when to walk alongside, and when to step away entirely.

This insight stemmed from choosing legacy over relevance. From understanding that leadership fulfills its purpose not when it is remembered, but when it is no longer needed.

> ***'The Legacy of Guidance'***
> *"Good leaders pave the way, lead the way,*
> *then walk away for others to walk the way."*

Conscious Breather

It reframes leadership as preparation, not permanence. It reflects on the responsibility of guiding others toward independence rather than attachment, and the discipline required to step aside once that work is done. It also affirms that the most enduring leaders are those who empower, release, and trust what they helped shape.

REFLECTIVE PAUSE: Take a beat, let that marinate and reach for acknowledgment without obligation. Think about the figures who shaped your thinking, directly or indirectly. The voices that once guided you when your own was still forming.

Reflect on this with care: Which guidance helped you grow, and which eventually needed to be released? Where did appreciation quietly turn into allegiance? How do you honor influence without surrendering authorship?

Guidance is meant to prepare, not possess. Its value is measured by how freely you can stand on your own. Let this remain present without pressure. Gratitude does not require permanence. Move on with this understanding, aware that the most enduring legacy of guidance is independence, not loyalty.

Forward Glance

Guidance fulfills its purpose the moment it becomes unnecessary. When direction gives way to self-trust, and presence is no longer required to sustain momentum, the work is complete. True legacy is not measured by loyalty retained, but by independence cultivated.

The quiet success of guidance is found not in being followed, but in being outgrown.

22

The Volume of Silence

The world we live in now is loud by design. The digital shift has handed everyone a voice, a platform, and an audience, however fleeting. Expression is no longer filtered by reflection, experience, or truth, but by immediacy. Most want to be heard, not necessarily understood. Presence matters more than substance, volume more than validity.

In this environment, extroversion has become the default posture. Opinions are shared instantly, reactions are rewarded, and silence is often mistaken for absence or indifference. ***The masses speak because they can, because they are expected to, because not speaking feels like falling behind.*** Noise multiplies itself, feeding on attention rather than meaning.

Yet a smaller number remain quiet. Not because they have nothing to say, but because they are aware of the weight of saying it. They wrestle with the urge to contribute, to correct, to respond, and choose restraint instead. Their silence is not passive, it is intentional. In a world addicted to output, remaining quiet becomes an act of design rather than deficiency.

Silence has never meant emptiness to me. As an ambivert, I learned early that quiet is not absence, but containment. I speak when there is something worth saying, and retreat when observation offers more truth than participation. To many, that restraint is misread as distance or disinterest. It is neither.

The longer I listened, the clearer it became that those who speak least often carry the most unprocessed noise within. ***Silence, when granted access, reveals its volume.*** The closer you are allowed to stand, the louder the inner world becomes, layered, restless, and alive with thought.

These thoughts emerged as a result of recognizing that presence does not require constant expression. Some minds communicate through stillness, revealing depth only to those patient enough to listen beyond words.

> ***'The Volume of Silence'***
> *"Don't be fooled by those of fewer words,*
> *as the closer you're allowed to get,*
> *the louder you'll hear their minds scream."*

Conscious Breather

It explores silence as a form of expression rather than absence. Through the lens of ambiversion, it reframes quiet as depth, containment, and discernment. It also affirms that restraint often conceals intensity, and that the truest understanding of another begins where words give way to listening.

```
REFLECTIVE PAUSE: Wait, take a minute to absorb that
and notice what isn't being said. Think about the
moments where silence carried more weight than
words. The pauses that revealed truth, tension, or
finality.

Reflect on this quietly: When did silence clarify
something you were avoiding? Where did absence of
response become an answer? How often do you rush to
fill space instead of listening to it?

Silence is not empty. It is dense with information.
Let this register without discomfort. What remains
unsaid often speaks most honestly. Move ahead with
this awareness, attentive to the meaning carried in
what is withheld as much as what is expressed.
```

Forward Glance

Silence is not absence, it is concentration. What remains unspoken often carries more truth than what is performed aloud. In a world that rewards constant expression, restraint becomes misread as distance. Yet those who listen deeply know that silence holds weight, discernment, and intent.

When words are chosen carefully, quiet becomes not a retreat, but a form of presence that needs no amplification.

23

Reaction: The Cause & Effect

Reaction is the default emotion most human beings live by. It arrives faster than thought, louder than reason, and often before awareness has a chance to intervene. We react to words, to tone, to perceived threat, to discomfort, to anything that disturbs equilibrium. It is not a moral flaw, but a human one, wired into survival and reinforced by habit.

How many times have you found yourself poised to react instantly, fingers hovering over a keyboard, pulse rising at a message, an email, a text, an accusation, an insult, or an implied blame?

In those moments, response feels urgent, almost compulsory, as if silence might equal weakness or agreement. Yet it is precisely in that immediacy that control is most easily surrendered, and where reactions often outrun understanding before consequence has a chance to be considered.

For much of my life, reaction felt justified. When triggered, responding immediately seemed honest, even necessary. ***I mistook speed for strength and expression for truth. It took time, and consequence, to realize how often reaction spoke before understanding had a chance to arrive.*** I began to notice a pattern. The more immediate the response, the less control I retained over the outcome.

Words once released could not be recalled, and actions taken in heat often created ripples far beyond their original cause. What felt like self-defense frequently became self-sabotage. This insight emerged later in life, when I finally learned the power of pause. To resist reaction is not suppression, it is authorship. Choosing if, when, and how to respond became an act of discipline, one that returned agency to where it belonged.

> ***'Reaction: The Cause & Effect'***
> *"Once triggered,*
> *resist the urge to react impulsively.*
> *Instead, pause, reflect, and craft*
> *a more thoughtful response, if at all.*
> *No reaction or a delayed reaction*
> *is almost always more prudent*
> *than an immediate reaction."*

Conscious Breather

This examines the long-term cost of impulsive response and the clarity that comes with restraint. It reflects on reaction as a learned behavior with lasting consequences, and reframes pause as power. It also affirms that control over reaction is control over trajectory, and that silence or delay often carries more wisdom than immediacy.

REFLECTIVE PAUSE: Let it settle in, slow down and observe the chain. Think about the situations where your reactions arrived before reflection. The moments where immediacy replaced intention.

Reflect on this honestly: What usually triggers your strongest responses? How often do you react to the present while arguing with the past? If you traced the effect backward, what cause would you find?

Reaction feels spontaneous, but it is rarely random. It follows patterns, rehearsals, and unexamined assumptions. Hold this awareness without self-criticism. Responsibility begins with recognition. Carry this forward as you continue, aware that changing outcomes often starts with interrupting the reaction itself.

Forward Glance

Reaction feels immediate, but its consequences are rarely contained. What is released in seconds often lingers far longer than intended, shaping outcomes that could have been avoided with pause. Between stimulus and response lies the only space where choice exists. To claim that space is not restraint for its own sake, it is responsibility.

And in learning to delay reaction, one begins to govern cause before it governs effect.

24

The Unspoken Command

True power rarely raises its voice. Presence carries a weight that volume never can. It does not need to announce itself, justify itself, or compete for attention. Power, when authentic, is felt before it is understood. It settles into a room quietly and reshapes the atmosphere without demanding acknowledgment.

Those who rely on volume often do so out of insecurity, not strength. Loud authority seeks compliance through force rather than respect, through interruption rather than influence. ***It confuses dominance with leadership, and noise with control. The louder the display, the more it reveals what is missing beneath it.***

The unspoken command lives in restraint. In the pause before speaking. In the certainty that does not need validation. It is authority rooted in self-assurance, not spectacle. And in a world saturated with noise, this kind of power becomes unmistakable precisely because it does not compete to be seen.

The most influential leaders I observed rarely raised their voice or asserted control. Their authority was felt long before it was declared. In brief moments when I found myself in similar positions, I understood why. True command does not announce itself, it settles into the room through clarity, consistency, and restraint.

There were instances where power was available to be exercised, yet choosing not to wield it proved more effective. Influence deepened when direction was implied rather than imposed. Respect followed presence, not enforcement. What initially felt counter intuitive revealed itself as the most stable form of leadership.

This reflection emerged from recognizing that authority weakens when it demands recognition. The strongest command is often the one never spoken.

> ***'The Unspoken Command'***
> *"He who possesses authority,*
> *never has the need to exercise it."*

Conscious Breather

Here, we explore authority as an internal posture rather than an external display. Drawing from lived moments of leadership, it affirms that true influence operates through presence, discipline, and restraint. It also reframes power as something that endures precisely because it does not need to be exercised to be felt.

```
REFLECTIVE PAUSE: Step back for a second and notice
the instructions you never agreed to. Think about
the expectations that shaped your behavior without
ever being voiced. The norms you followed to avoid
friction rather than because they aligned with you.

Reflect on this carefully: What rules have you been
obeying simply because they were implied? Where did
compliance feel safer than curiosity? How often did
silence signal instruction rather than freedom?

Unspoken commands are powerful because they
masquerade as choice. They persist not through
force, but through assumption. Let this remain
present without defensiveness. Awareness is the
first interruption. Move on with this understanding,
attentive to what you follow, and why, even when no
one asks you to.
```

Forward Glance

Authority that needs to be announced has already weakened. The most enduring influence moves quietly, shaping direction without coercion or display. When presence carries clarity and restraint governs action, command becomes implicit rather than imposed. What follows is not obedience, but alignment.

And in that space, power no longer needs a voice to be understood.

25

Where Light Meets Thought

How open-minded are you? And how open-minded are the people around you? We often assume we can spot it easily, mistaking confidence for clarity and agreement for openness. Yet an open mind is not revealed by what someone claims to believe, but by how they respond when those beliefs are challenged.

Can you recognize the difference between curiosity and defensiveness, between inquiry and dismissal? What instrument do you use to measure openness, your comfort, your certainty, or your willingness to remain engaged when clarity disrupts familiarity? These questions are not designed to test intelligence, but humility. For light only enters where thought is willing to receive it.

An open mind is often mistaken for agreement. In reality, it is a willingness to let ideas pass through without immediately resisting or adopting them. These glimpses exist because I learned to sit with contradiction, to examine beliefs without rushing to defend them, and to allow light to reach places thought once kept closed.

As that openness grew, so did an unexpected awareness. I began to encounter minds so sealed that even clarity failed to penetrate them. Not in darkness or confusion, but in full daylight, where evidence was visible and questions were simple. Some do not reject truth because it is hidden, but because it threatens the comfort of what they already know.

Light does not erase darkness by force, it reveals it by presence. Thought, when allowed to remain open, becomes illumination rather than confinement. When it refuses, even the brightest clarity becomes invisible.

> ***'Where Light Meets Thought'***
> *"Closed minds wander endlessly in shadows,*
> *while open minds embrace the light,*
> *even in the darkness of night."*

Conscious Breather

It affirms open-mindedness as an active discipline grounded in humility and courage. It contrasts the evolution of thought with the stagnation of certainty, revealing how some minds remain closed even in the presence of clarity. It also positions openness as the gateway through which understanding enters, and without which light itself cannot be seen.

```
REFLECTIVE PAUSE: Stop, maybe turn the lights out
and allow clarity to land. Now, think about the
```

moments when understanding didn't arrive through force, but through quiet alignment. When something complex suddenly felt simple, not because it was explained, but because it was seen.

Reflect on this softly: When has insight arrived without struggle? What became clear once you stopped trying to convince yourself? How often does truth appear when you stop resisting it?

Light doesn't argue. It reveals. Let this awareness settle without urgency. Illumination rarely demands action, only honesty. Carry this forward as you continue, allowing clarity to guide rather than overwhelm what comes next.

Forward Glance

Light does not force its way into the mind, it waits to be allowed in. Thought determines whether clarity is received or resisted. An open mind is not proven by what it accepts, but by what it is willing to examine without defensiveness. When light meets thought without obstruction, understanding expands naturally.

And when it does not, it is not because light was absent, but because thought chose to remain closed.

VI

Moral Sovereignty

The 'Quiet Authority', undoubtedly leads us to center on sovereignty of mind and moral self-governance. These reflections explore intellect, responsibility, and the unseen laws that return intention to the self. Power is internalized, ethics self-authored, and connection reshaped through accountability. Wisdom here emerges as alignment between thought, action, and consequence.

As you approach it, consider where responsibility has been claimed fully, and where it has quietly been deferred.

26

The Sovereign Mind

How sovereign is your mind, truly? And how sovereign are the minds you move among each day? It is easy to believe our thoughts are our own, until they are questioned. Until a headline provokes reaction, a crowd demands alignment, or a familiar narrative goes unchallenged simply because it is familiar.

What measures do we use to determine independence of thought? Is it the ability to repeat an argument convincingly, or the willingness to examine where it came from? Can one tell the difference between a conclusion reached and one inherited?

A sovereign mind is not defined by defiance, but by discernment, the capacity to think freely even when conformity feels safer.

In a world saturated with opinion, outrage, and manufactured certainty, independent thought has become quietly endangered. Information moves faster than reflection, and narratives are often accepted not because they are true, but because they are repeated.

I came to realize that while society may influence what we are exposed to, it cannot govern how we think unless we surrender that authority willingly. ***The sovereign mind is not loud or reactionary. It observes before it aligns, questions before it adopts, and resists the pressure to outsource judgment to crowds, algorithms, or inherited belief systems.***

In an age that rewards conformity disguised as consensus, thinking for oneself has become a subtle act of defiance. This reflection emerged from witnessing how easily intellect is shaped by fear, identity, and repetition.

Sovereignty begins where discernment is reclaimed, and where thought is treated not as a tool for division, but as a responsibility.

> ***The Sovereign Mind'***
> *"We are born with the powers of thought and intellect.*
> *Society will attempt to shape our thoughts*
> *but can never control our intellect.*
> *Use both with wisdom."*

Conscious Breather

It examines intellectual independence in an era of pervasive influence and collective conditioning. It affirms the right and duty to govern one's own thinking, resisting external pressures that seek compliance over clarity. It frames sovereignty not as isolation, but as disciplined self-authorship in a world increasingly hostile to independent thought.

REFLECTIVE PAUSE: Soak that up, slow down and notice where your thinking begins. Think about the moments you deferred your judgment, not out of respect, but out of habit. The times you borrowed certainty instead of building it.

Reflect on this with clarity: Where have you outsourced your thinking? When did agreement feel easier than inquiry? What changes when your mind answers first to itself?

Sovereignty is not isolation. It is responsibility. Let this remain present without resistance. A self-governed mind does not reject influence, it chooses it. Move ahead with this awareness, grounded in the understanding that autonomy begins where discernment is exercised deliberately.

Forward Glance

A sovereign mind does not shout its independence, it practices it. It remains intact amid noise, unmoved by pressure to conform or perform allegiance. True sovereignty is exercised in discernment, in the refusal to surrender judgment for comfort or belonging. When thought is governed from within, influence loses its hold.

And in that freedom, the mind answers only to truth, not to the crowd.

27

The Mirror of Morality

Human behavior often bends toward certainty. We prefer the comfort of being right, the quiet authority it grants us, and the protection it offers our self-image. Admitting fault feels like surrender, as though error diminishes our worth rather than refines it. So we defend our positions, justify our actions, and polish our narratives until they shine just enough to keep doubt at bay.

Yet within this resistance lies an overlooked power. The moment we allow the possibility of being wrong, not as failure but as awareness, we reclaim agency. ***To recognize a wrong is not to be weakened by it, but to gain the rare chance to correct it.*** Morality does not demand perfection, it asks for honesty. And it is only through that honesty that growth, repair, and true accountability can begin.

Morality stopped feeling absolute the moment I accepted my own contradictions. I learned that being human means getting things wrong, sometimes with the best of intentions.

What mattered was not the illusion of righteousness, but the willingness to look honestly at my actions without outsourcing judgment or blame.

I came to understand that no one truly has the power to make me right or wrong. That responsibility lives inward. ***Each mistake became less a mark of failure and more a prompt to correct, to realign, to do better next time.*** Moral clarity did not arrive as certainty, but as accountability.

This reflection emerged from abandoning the need to appear correct and choosing instead to remain correctable. To face oneself without defense is uncomfortable, but it is the only place where integrity survives.

This one's a real tongue twister. Twisted as it may seem, it captures what I genuinely believe to be my right.

> ***'The Mirror of Morality'***
> *"Nobody can wrong or right me,*
> *as I long to be right,*
> *only to right my wrongs,*
> *as that's my given right*
> *even though I might be wrong."*

Conscious Breather

Here we explore ethics as an internal reckoning rather than an external verdict. It frames morality as a personal discipline shaped by reflection, responsibility, and the courage to acknowledge error. It also affirms that being human is not about moral perfection, but about the ongoing commitment to right one's wrongs when they are revealed.

```
REFLECTIVE PAUSE: Give that a moment to land and
look inward. Think about the standards you apply
most firmly. Not the ones you defend publicly, but
the ones you live by when no one is watching.

Reflect on this with care: Where do your actions
align with your values, and where do they quietly
diverge? What do you excuse in yourself that you
condemn in others? When did justification replace
integrity?

Morality is not tested in theory. It is revealed in
private. Let this register without self-protection.
The mirror does not accuse, it reflects. Carry this
forward as you continue, aware that ethical clarity
begins with unfiltered self-examination.
```

Forward Glance

Morality reveals itself most clearly when no one else is watching. It is not shaped by applause or punishment, but by the willingness to face one's own reflection without distortion. Judgment loses its authority when responsibility is claimed internally. The mirror does not accuse, it simply reflects.

And what we choose to correct after looking into it determines who we become.

28

The Law of Reflection

Karma is often misunderstood as a system of cosmic justice, a ledger of good and bad deeds waiting to be balanced. In reality, it operates far more quietly and far more immediately. It is not about fate keeping score, but about life responding in kind.

What we put into the world has a way of finding its way back, not because it must, but because it mirrors us.

The Law of Reflection works through alignment, not consequence. ***Energy, intention, and behavior shape the environments we move through and the responses we receive. We are reflected back to ourselves through people, circumstances, and outcomes, often without realizing that we initiated the exchange.*** What feels like coincidence is frequently consistency.

Seen this way, Karma is not something that happens to us later. It is something we are participating in constantly.

Every interaction leaves an imprint. Every choice sets a tone. The world does not judge us, it reflects us. And once this becomes visible, responsibility shifts from fear of consequence to awareness of creation.

At an individual level, many eventually recognize that what we project outward often finds its way back to us. But has society reached that same understanding? Have we truly grasped that tone, intention, and conduct do not vanish once released, but circulate, shaping the very environments we later complain about?

We speak of consequences as though they are imposed from above, yet rarely acknowledge how collective behavior manufactures collective outcomes. If reflection is a law rather than a metaphor, then the question becomes unavoidable: are we living in the mirror of what we have created, and if so, are we willing to change what we send forward?

For a long time, I measured events by what they brought to me. With age came a quieter realization: much of what returns to us is shaped by what we first project outward. ***Tone invites tone. Intention echoes intention. Whether we like it or not, we participate in the atmosphere we later move through.***

There were moments I could trace outcomes back to my own posture, my words, my presence. Not with blame, but with clarity. Reflection is not punishment, it is feedback. Life responds honestly, even when we are not ready to receive the response.

This reflection emerged from the desire to play it forward, to move with awareness of how small choices ripple beyond the immediate moment. What we offer does not disappear, it circulates.

> ***'The Law of Reflection'***
> *"Good or otherwise, everything brought upon us*
> *is a reflection of what we bring to those around us"*

Conscious Breather

It examines the reciprocal nature of action and outcome. It frames life as a mirror that responds to intention, conduct, and energy over time. It also affirms responsibility as empowerment, encouraging mindful contribution in the hope that what is given forward returns with integrity and purpose.

REFLECTIVE PAUSE: This is an ancient concept almost in reverse. So, examine what returns to you. Think about the patterns you keep encountering. The behaviors, reactions, or outcomes that seem to echo back in different forms.

Reflect on this honestly: What do these repetitions suggest about what you project? Where might response be mirroring intention? How often do you search for causes outward instead of inward?

Reflection is not punishment. It is feedback. Let this awareness settle without resistance. Understanding the mirror changes what it reflects. Move on with this understanding, knowing that what you send forward often determines what finds its way back.

Forward Glance

Reflection does not pause at the individual, it scales. What is projected outward returns not only to the sender, but to the environment it enters. Societies, like people, live inside the consequences of what they repeatedly express, reward, and tolerate. If the world feels fractured, volatile, or harsh, it is worth asking what has been normalized long enough to feel invisible.

The mirror does not discriminate. It returns what it is given, patiently and precisely.

29

The Evolution of Connection

One of the quieter truths we all come to accept is that timing governs connection as much as intention does. Sometimes people are simply not ready to allow others into their journey. Not out of malice, but out of fear, distraction, or unfinished work within themselves. In those seasons, presence is overlooked, effort goes unnoticed, and connection remains one-sided.

What is rarely acknowledged is that readiness has a cost. By the time some are prepared to open the door, the very people they once ignored have continued forward, changed by time, distance, and growth. Not in resentment, but in alignment. Connection, like all living things, evolves. It cannot be paused, preserved, or reclaimed on demand. When paths cross again, they often do so as different selves, shaped by choices made while waiting or moving on.

For much of my life, connection felt conditional. ***From early rejection to adult estrangement, belonging often seemed tied***

to versions of myself I was expected to perform rather than who I was allowed to be. I learned early how to adapt, how to fit just enough to remain close, while quietly editing parts of myself to preserve access.

As time passed, roles reversed. Children grew, identities solidified, and I began to recognize a shift I could no longer ignore. The distance I once feared became discernment. The need to belong gave way to the right to choose where and with whom I connected. What once felt like rejection revealed itself as redirection.

This reflection emerged from that turning point. From realizing that people do not change as much as the meaning of connection does. Growth rearranges proximity.

> ***'The Evolution of Connection'***
> *"Once upon a time,*
> *I did not belong in your world.*
> *Today, you no longer belong in mine.*
> *People don't change,*
> *change changes people."*

Conscious Breather

It explores how belonging transforms across a lifetime. It traces the journey from seeking acceptance to choosing alignment, and reframes rejection as a catalyst for clarity. It also affirms that connection evolves not through sameness, but through self-respect, and that change does not alter people, it alters who belongs where.

REFLECTIVE PAUSE: Think about that for a second and look at how your connections have changed. Think about the people who once felt essential, and those who arrived later with quieter significance. The relationships that evolved, softened, or naturally released.

Reflect on this with openness: How have your needs in connection shifted over time? Which bonds deepened through honesty rather than proximity? Where did distance create clarity instead of loss?

Connection is not static. It grows, adapts, and sometimes concludes. Let this remain present without nostalgia. Change in connection does not diminish what was real. Carry this forward as you move on, aware that meaningful connection honors both closeness and evolution.

Forward Glance

Connection does not fail as often as it simply moves out of sync. Readiness cannot be forced, and presence cannot be preserved on pause. When paths diverge, it is rarely because care was absent, but because growth continued in different directions. What once felt like rejection reveals itself, over time, as alignment asserting itself.

The evolution of connection is not about holding on, but about recognizing when closeness has served its purpose and allowing distance to do the rest.

30

Dawn to Dusk Illuminated

There was a passage I once encountered that reframed gratitude in a way that stayed with me. It suggested that gratitude is not merely a response to abundance, but the condition that allows abundance to multiply. That whoever practices gratitude will be given more, while the absence of it quietly erodes even what is already present. At the time, it felt less like a promise and more like a principle.

What resonated was not the idea of reward, but the mechanism. Gratitude sharpens awareness. It trains the mind to recognize what exists rather than fixate on what is missing.

Over time, I noticed that days anchored in appreciation expanded, while those approached with indifference contracted. The practice did not change circumstances overnight, but it altered how much of life I was actually able to receive.

This insight reinforced my daily ritual. Gratitude at dawn opened perception. Gratitude at dusk preserved perspective.

And in that rhythm, abundance revealed itself not as accumulation, but as attention.

I learned that days do not improve by chance, they are shaped by how they are entered and how they are released. Mornings set a tone long before the world makes its demands, and nights quietly decide what we carry forward. Gratitude became less of an emotion and more of a discipline, practiced deliberately at both edges of the day.

Beginning each morning with acknowledgment steadied me. Not for what I hoped would happen, but for what already existed. Ending each night with reflection softened what the day had taken. Even on difficult days, this simple rhythm created continuity, a way to remain anchored regardless of circumstance.

This reflection grew out of repetition. A daily choice to illuminate the day from both ends, allowing gratitude to frame experience rather than react to it.

> ***'Dawn to Dusk Illuminated'***
> *"Life only prospers when you start each day*
> *with an attitude of gratitude,*
> *and end every night in a positive light."*

Conscious Breather

This presents gratitude as a daily practice that bookends life with intention. It reframes appreciation as rhythm rather than reaction, affirming that how one begins and ends the day determines its emotional clarity. It also honors consistency as the quiet force that turns ordinary days into grounded ones.

REFLECTIVE PAUSE: A glaringly simple concept to consider a pause and take in the full arc. Think about the cycles you've lived through. Beginnings that felt uncertain, middles that tested endurance, endings that arrived without ceremony.

Reflect on this gently: Where did clarity arrive gradually rather than all at once? What did persistence teach you that urgency never could? If today were complete, what would feel illuminated rather than unfinished?

Illumination does not require spectacle. It reveals itself through continuity. Let this remain present without urgency. Some understanding is meant to be lived with, not resolved. Move ahead with this awareness, carrying the quiet knowing that comes from having witnessed the whole span.

Forward Glance

Gratitude does not wait for life to improve, it improves how life is received. When the day is met with acknowledgment and released with reflection, experience is framed rather than endured. What begins in awareness carries through action, and what ends in appreciation restores balance. From dawn to dusk, attention determines abundance.

And in honoring the day at both edges, life quietly offers more of itself in return.

VII

Alignment Over Applause

After 'Moral Sovereignty', we examine value over visibility, worth above validation and evolution beyond convention.
These reflections explore fortune's elusiveness, empathy earned rather than assumed, intention as gravity, and integrity as liberation.
Progress here is measured by alignment, not applause, and growth requires the courage to move against momentum without losing oneself.
Once inside, consider where validation has shaped your path, and where alignment has quietly been neglected.

31

The Invisibility of Fortune

There was a period in my life where everything appeared to be working. Momentum was steady, opportunities aligned, and effort seemed to meet reward without resistance. From the outside, it looked like thriving. From the inside, it felt earned, stable, almost dependable. And then, without warning, it was gone.

What vanished did not fade gradually, it collapsed swiftly. Structures I assumed were solid revealed how provisional they truly were. Relationships shifted. Certainties dissolved. What I had built over years was stripped away in moments, leaving behind an unfamiliar quiet.

In that stillness, I learned how invisible fortune truly is, present until it isn't, dependable only in hindsight.

That experience recalibrated everything. It taught me not to anchor identity, confidence, or peace to conditions that can evaporate overnight. ***Thriving had masked fragility. Loss***

revealed truth. And in that truth, resilience replaced reliance, and awareness took the place of assumption.

It took reaching the halfway mark of life to understand how unreliable fortune truly is. For years, I chased signs of it, moments when things aligned effortlessly, when progress felt smooth and reward appeared predictable. What I failed to see then was that fortune is most present when it goes unnoticed, and most absent when it becomes the focus.

I watched opportunities arrive quietly and vanish just as silently, often unrelated to effort or merit. What I once called luck revealed itself as timing, awareness, and preparedness intersecting briefly. The moment I tried to hold onto it, to name it, measure it, or expect it, it slipped away.

This insight arose from learning that fortune favors attention, not pursuit. It shows itself when humility replaces entitlement, and disappears when assumed. The lesson was not to rely on fortune, but to cultivate steadiness without it.

> ***'The Invisibility of Fortune'***
> *"Good fortune appears when you're not looking*
> *and disappears when you're not thinking."*

Conscious Breather

This reflects on the elusive nature of luck and timing, revealed through lived experience at life's midpoint. It reframes fortune as fleeting and conditional, shaped by awareness rather than control. It also affirms that resilience, presence, and preparation matter more than chance, and that true stability is built independently of fortune's arrival or absence.

REFLECTIVE PAUSE: A little depth here that requires a pause to look at what you may have overlooked. Think about the forms of fortune that didn't announce themselves. The quiet consistencies, the unnoticed stability, the absence of certain struggles.

Reflect on this thoughtfully: What has supported you without demanding recognition Where did you mistake normalcy for lack? How often did you measure fortune only by what was visible or dramatic?

Fortune rarely arrives as spectacle. More often, it hides in continuity. Let this awareness settle without comparison. Not everything valuable declares itself loudly. Carry this forward as you continue, attentive to the quiet advantages that shape a life without ever asking to be seen.

Forward Glance

Fortune is never as solid as it appears, nor as absent as it feels in its departure. What arrives without warning can vanish just as quickly, indifferent to effort, merit, or intention. When everything is stripped away in an instant, what remains becomes unmistakably clear. Stability was never meant to be found in fortune itself, but in the capacity to stand without it.

And once that is learned, loss no longer defines the fall, it reveals the ground beneath.

32

The Measure of Worthiness

People crave empathy and society has learned to impose it. Not through understanding, but through outward displays of need, suffering, or grievance, whether seen publicly or carried quietly in private. Attention becomes the currency, and pity, its shorthand. The louder or more visible the struggle, the faster empathy is expected, often without context, discernment, or truth.

In this climate, empathy shifts from a human response to a social obligation. We are encouraged to feel before we are allowed to question. To validate before we are permitted to understand.

The measure of worthiness becomes externalized, determined not by character or responsibility, but by presentation. Pain, when displayed convincingly enough, is assumed to justify behavior, absolve accountability, or demand exception.

What gets lost is the difference between compassion and concession. Empathy offered without clarity does not elevate, it enables. ***The 'Measure of Worthiness' asks a harder question, not who is hurting, but how we respond without surrendering judgment, integrity, or truth.*** Because empathy that bypasses discernment may soothe the moment, but it rarely serves growth.

Empathy has often been mistaken for obligation. Because I do not offer it freely or indiscriminately, I have been branded as distant, cold, even indifferent. What is rarely seen is the discipline behind that restraint. I do not lack empathy, I guard it.

Experience taught me that empathy given without discernment is quickly depleted or exploited. I learned to measure worthiness not by entitlement or demand, but by conduct, consistency, and character. To extend deep understanding where it is neither respected nor reciprocated is not compassion, it is erosion.

This reflection emerged from standing firm in that distinction. Empathy, when offered deliberately, retains its power. When reserved for those who honor it, it becomes meaningful rather than performative.

> ***'The Measure of Worthiness'***
> *"Empathy is a deep and vulnerable emotion*
> *reserved for those I deem worthy,*
> *not those who deem themselves worthy."*

Conscious Breather

This reframes empathy as a finite and intentional resource rather than an unlimited obligation. It challenges the assumption that emotional availability must be universal, and affirms discernment as a form of self-respect. It also positions selective empathy not as coldness, but as clarity shaped by experience and integrity.

REFLECTIVE PAUSE: Take as many moments as needed, pause and examine the scale you've been using. Think about how you've measured your own worth over time. The milestones, validations, comparisons, or approvals that quietly set the standard.

Reflect on this carefully: Who taught you what was worthy of recognition? Where did achievement become a substitute for self-regard? What remains of your worth when nothing is being measured?

Worthiness is often inherited before it is questioned. Many spend their lives trying to earn what was never conditional. Let this register without judgment. Releasing false measures does not diminish value, it reveals it. Carry this forward as you move on, aware that worth is not proven by accumulation, but affirmed by presence.

Forward Glance

Worthiness is not determined by proximity, pressure, or persistence. It reveals itself through conduct, consistency, and respect for what is given. Empathy offered without discernment diminishes both giver and receiver. When care is reserved for those who honor it, it retains its depth and meaning. ***The measure is not how much is extended, but whether what is extended is received with integrity.***

33

Evolving Beyond Convention

Society often speaks of change as though it belongs to someone else. A movement, a generation, a moment yet to arrive. We wait for revolutions, for loud gestures and sweeping reforms, while excusing our own stillness. In doing so, we overlook the most effective form of evolution, the quiet kind.

Change does not require spectacle to be real. It begins privately, in daily decisions, in the refusal to repeat what no longer serves, in the courage to behave differently without announcement or permission. ***A single adjusted mindset alters conduct. Altered conduct reshapes influence. Over time, quiet shifts accumulate into visible progress.***

This reflection arose from recognizing that evolution is not an event, but a practice. Responsibility does not sit with the crowd, it rests with the individual. And often, the most enduring change arrives not through revolution, but through consistency carried forward in silence.

Convention offers comfort by promising belonging, structure, and predictability. For a time, it serves a purpose. But what stabilizes one season can quietly suffocate the next. I learned that staying loyal to outdated norms out of habit is not discipline, it is stagnation.

Evolution does not require rejection of everything that came before, only the courage to question what no longer fits. Progress, when honest, demands movement, not loyalty to form. The moment convention becomes identity, growth becomes a threat. Remaining static may feel safe, but it carries a long-term cost, the erosion of relevance, integrity, and self-authorship.

This reflection dawned from choosing adaptability over attachment. To evolve is not to rebel, but to respond intelligently to change without losing one's core.

> ***'Evolving Beyond Convention'***
> *"Revolution is the evolution of convention.*
> *The challenge is to constantly change,*
> *to avoid becoming a victim of either."*

Conscious Breather

It examines growth as a continuous process that requires reassessment rather than allegiance. It challenges rigid adherence to tradition and reframes evolution as an act of awareness and responsibility. It also affirms that true progress lies in knowing when to honor convention and when to move beyond it, without fear or apology.

REFLECTIVE PAUSE: Just take that in and reflect on what has always been considered normal. Think about the rules you followed simply because they were established. The paths presented as sensible, respectable, or inevitable.

Reflect on this carefully: Which conventions did you accept without ever choosing? Where did belonging take priority over alignment? What parts of you stayed quiet in order to fit the shape you were given?

Convention survives through repetition, not relevance. It persists because it feels safer than uncertainty. Let this awareness remain present without rebellion. Growth does not require opposition, only discernment. Move ahead with this understanding, aware that evolution begins the moment conformity stops being mistaken for stability.

Forward Glance

Convention persists not because it is right, but because it is familiar. Change is often deferred, assigned to movements, leaders, or generations yet to come, while personal responsibility is quietly excused. Yet evolution does not require rebellion or revolution to begin. It starts in private choices, in the refusal to repeat what no longer fits, and in the courage to act differently without announcement.

When enough individuals evolve quietly, convention changes without ever noticing how it happened.

34

The Gravity of Intention

Most of us can recall moments when we wished fervently for something, convinced it would bring relief, validation, or resolution. With hindsight, many of those desires reveal themselves as misaligned, born from impatience, ego, or fear rather than wisdom. The saying "B***e careful what you wish for, you might just get it***" endures because it is painfully accurate.

Intention does not distinguish between what serves us and what simply satisfies a want. When desire is unchecked, it sets forces in motion that deliver outcomes without regard for readiness or consequence.

I have watched wishes arrive exactly as imagined, only to discover they carried costs I had not accounted for. The lesson was not to stop wanting, but to become more conscious of what was being invited into my life. This insight stemmed from understanding that intention is already an act of creation. Before outcome appears, responsibility is already present.

It took time to understand that intention carries weight long before action does. What we hold inward, what we wish for, what we silently rehearse, already begins to shape the field around us.

I learned this not through theory, but through consequence. Through watching outcomes unfold that felt disproportionate, yet perfectly aligned with what had been set in motion beneath awareness.

Intention does not negotiate. Once formed, it exerts pull, drawing people, circumstances, and reactions into its orbit. Even well-meaning desires carry consequence, and not all intentions land where we imagine they will. The mistake is believing that only action creates impact. Thought, when charged with desire, already bends reality.

This contemplation emerged from realizing that responsibility begins earlier than behavior. It begins at conception, in the quiet moment where intention is chosen or left unchecked.

> ***The Gravity of Intention'***
> *"Good or otherwise,*
> *be mindful of what you wish for*
> *as everything comes with consequences.*
> *Thoughts are similar to Newton's law:*
> *for every thought or action,*
> *there's an equal but opposite*
> *thought or reaction."*

Conscious Breather

Here we explore intention as an unseen force that shapes outcome as reliably as action. It reframes thought as consequential, carrying momentum and responsibility long before results appear. It also affirms awareness as essential, urging discernment not only in what we do, but in what we intend, knowing that every intention sets something in motion.

REFLECTIVE PAUSE: A little scientific. So, stop and notice what pulls you. Think about the intentions that quietly shaped your direction. Not the ones you announced, but the ones you carried consistently.

Reflect on this with honesty: What have your repeated choices been pointing toward? Where did intention outweigh circumstance? If your actions had a center of gravity, what would it reveal?

Intention does not need volume to be powerful. It works through consistency, not declaration. Let this remain present without justification. Direction is often chosen long before it is acknowledged. Carry this forward as you continue, aware that what you intend steadily shapes what you become.

Forward Glance

Intention does not wait for action to matter. Once formed, it begins to pull, shaping direction long before outcome appears. Wishes made without awareness still carry consequence, and desire left unchecked does not ask whether it serves us. What gives intention its weight is not its purity, but its persistence.

To choose intention carefully is to accept responsibility early, before momentum decides on our behalf.

35

Liberation Through Integrity

We live in a society that too often confuses fortune with merit. Those with less are shamed for their position, ridiculed for their struggle, or dismissed as though circumstance were character. Possession becomes proof, and absence becomes accusation. It is an unkind arithmetic, one that assigns worth based on what is visible rather than what is endured.

I learned early that integrity demands resistance to this mindset. Having more does not make one more deserving, just as having less does not make one lesser. To stand beside those labeled failures or outcasts is not charity, it is recognition of shared humanity. Bullying the vulnerable under the guise of superiority reveals nothing about strength, only fear and moral vacancy.

Liberation, I found, is not found in aligning with advantage, but in standing firmly with dignity, especially when the world encourages you to look away.

Since I can remember, I found myself drawn to those pushed to the margins. Not out of defiance, but recognition. The ones labeled inconvenient, unpopular, or difficult often carried truths that made others uncomfortable. Standing beside them came at a cost, exclusion, misunderstanding, and quiet judgment, but it never felt like a sacrifice.

Integrity revealed itself early as alignment, not approval. Choosing who to include became a reflection of who I was willing to be. Exclusion in exchange for belonging never appealed to me. I learned that inclusion rooted in conscience is liberating, even when it isolates.

This insight emerged from that constancy. From understanding that being excluded for one's values is far less confining than being included for one's silence.

> ***'Liberation Through Integrity'***
> *"To be excluded because of who I include,*
> *is far more liberating than to be included*
> *because of who I exclude."*

Conscious Breather

This explores integrity as a deliberate commitment to principle over acceptance. It reflects on lifelong solidarity with the marginalized and reframes exclusion as freedom when it preserves conscience. It also affirms that true liberation is found not in fitting in, but in standing firm beside those one refuses to abandon.

REFLECTIVE PAUSE: Hold here and assess your alignment. Think about the moments when telling the truth cost you comfort. The times integrity required something to be surrendered.

Reflect on this carefully: Where did honesty narrow your options but expand your peace? What did you stop tolerating once you stopped compromising yourself? If no one rewarded your integrity, would you still choose it?

Integrity does not liberate by force. It frees through coherence. Let this register without expectation. Freedom earned this way does not need witnesses. Move ahead with this awareness, grounded in the understanding that liberation is sustained not by escape, but by consistency with yourself.

Forward Glance

Integrity liberates because it refuses to participate in cruelty, even when cruelty is normalized. In a world that shames the less fortunate and equates possession with worth, standing firm beside dignity becomes an act of resistance. To measure humanity by circumstance is to misunderstand it entirely. Liberation is not found in aligning with advantage, but in refusing to abandon conscience for comfort.

And once integrity is chosen, no hierarchy has the power to diminish it.

VIII

The Honest Turn

The 'Alignment Over Applause' leads us to confront the moral inflection points that define inner freedom. These reflections explore conscience, guilt, admission, doubt, and the courage required to face oneself without disguise.

Wisdom here moves beyond being right, liberation begins with honesty, and guidance emerges through vulnerability.

As you cross the threshold, ask yourself where truth has been avoided for comfort, and what freedom might follow if it were chosen instead?

36

The Betrayal of Conscience

For reasons that are rarely examined, humanity has developed a deep and persistent relationship with guilt. Not the kind that follows wrongdoing, but the kind that appears simply for choosing oneself, for saying no, for stepping away, or for refusing to comply. This guilt often surfaces before any harm is done, urging us to act against our own better judgment.

We feel it when we stay in a job that drains us because leaving feels disloyal. When we maintain relationships that repeatedly cross boundaries because distance feels cruel. When we agree to expectations we never consented to, just to avoid disappointing someone else.

Parents feel guilty for prioritizing their well-being. Children feel guilty for becoming independent. Employees feel guilty for resting. Friends feel guilty for outgrowing dynamics that no longer fit.

In each case, guilt masquerades as virtue, but functions as control. It pressures us to override intuition, silence discernment, and betray our own clarity in favor of comfort, approval, or familiarity. What is framed as kindness often becomes self-abandonment.

This insight arose from recognizing that guilt is not always a moral signal. More often, it is the residue of conditioning, activated when conscience tries to assert truth in environments that reward compliance. The betrayal occurs not when we feel guilt, but when we obey it without question.

We like to believe that conscience fails loudly, through dramatic moral collapse or deliberate wrongdoing. In truth, it is usually betrayed in smaller moments, the ones we justify, postpone, or quietly excuse. I have learned that most compromises are not forced, they are permitted.

There were times I knew better and still chose convenience. ***Times when guilt didn't arrive after the fact, but before the action, offering a warning I chose to soften or ignore. That inner friction was never confusion, it was clarity asking to be honored. Each time it wasn't, something subtle shifted.*** Not enough to break me, but enough to dull the edge of integrity.

This understanding arose from recognizing how universal that pattern is. We all bargain with conscience, convincing ourselves that this once doesn't count, that context absolves intent, that silence is neutral. It isn't.

> ***'The Betrayal of Conscience'***
> *"Guilt will always compel you*
> *to act against your better judgment."*

Conscious Breather

This examines the quiet ways we act against our better judgment, knowingly or unknowingly. It reframes guilt as an early signal rather than a punishment, and exposes compromise as a cumulative act. It also affirms that conscience is not lost through ignorance, but through repeated dismissal, and that integrity is preserved by listening the first time truth speaks.

```
REFLECTIVE PAUSE:  Without guilt, take a brief
pause, reflect and look at where you looked away.
Think about the times you sensed something was
wrong, yet continued anyway. Not out of malice, but
out of convenience, fear, or exhaustion.

Reflect on this with care: When did you first notice
the dissonance? What justification helped you move
past it? How long did it take before silence felt
heavier than resistance?

Conscience rarely disappears. It waits. Let this
register without self-punishment. Recognition is not
condemnation, it is an opening. Carry this forward
as you move on, aware that reconciliation with
conscience begins the moment honesty replaces
avoidance.
```

Forward Glance

Conscience rarely disappears, it is negotiated away in small, repeated moments. Guilt often arrives not because we acted wrongly, but because we knew better and chose otherwise. Each compromise feels minor in isolation, yet over time they accumulate into distance from self. Betrayal is not a single act, but a pattern of avoidance.

And integrity is restored not by grand correction, but by listening the first time truth speaks.

37

Wisdom Beyond Victory

There is a quiet impulse in all of us to want to be right, even when the cost is visible and avoidable. We pursue correctness as validation, as proof of intelligence, superiority, or moral standing, rarely pausing to consider the collateral damage. Words sharpened to win often leave wounds that outlast the argument itself. Gloating may feel brief and satisfying, but its impact on the other can linger as shame, resentment, or withdrawal long after the moment has passed.

I had to confront how easily being right can become an act of harm. Accuracy does not grant permission to humiliate, diminish, or dominate. The challenge is not in seeing clearly, but in holding that clarity with restraint. Humility in being right means recognizing that truth does not require triumph, and that correction offered without care can become cruelty.

Wisdom does not announce itself through victory. It reveals itself through mercy, through silence when silence preserves dignity, and through the discipline to value relationship over recognition, even when another is wrong.

There were moments when I was proven right and felt no satisfaction in it. No relief, no triumph, no sense of arrival. Instead, there was an unexpected heaviness in watching others bear the cost of being wrong. Clarity, when it arrives alone, can feel isolating rather than affirming.

I learned that being right does not always serve connection, and winning an argument rarely restores balance. Insight without compassion sharpens division. There is a loneliness that comes with seeing consequences unfold exactly as predicted, especially when those consequences harm people you would rather protect than correct.

This contemplation was inspired by choosing restraint over validation. From realizing that wisdom is not measured by accuracy alone, but by the care taken with what that accuracy reveals.

> ***'Wisdom Beyond Victory'***
> *"One should take no comfort in being right,*
> *as there's greater discomfort in others being wrong."*

Conscious Breather

It explores the emotional and ethical weight of being right when others are wrong. It reframes correctness as responsibility rather than achievement, and challenges the impulse to seek validation through outcome. It also affirms that true wisdom lies not in winning, but in holding truth with humility, empathy, and restraint.

REFLECTIVE PAUSE: Take it all in. Reconsider what winning has meant to you. Think about the moments where being right mattered more than being at peace. The arguments won, the positions defended, the satisfaction that faded faster than expected.

Reflect on this with honesty: What did victory cost you that wasn't visible at the time? Where did insisting on winning prevent understanding from forming? If no one kept score, what would you choose instead?

Wisdom does not seek the podium. It looks for clarity. Let this awareness settle without regret. Outgrowing the need to win is not loss, it is expansion. Carry this forward as you continue, aware that the deepest insight often arrives when the contest ends.

Forward Glance

Being right carries weight when it arrives without joy. Accuracy that wounds others leaves a residue no victory can erase. The desire to win often speaks louder than the responsibility to care, yet wisdom asks for the opposite discipline.

To hold truth without gloating, to recognize consequence without exploiting it, and to choose humility even when correctness is assured, this is where wisdom moves beyond victory and into humanity.

38

Admission Is Free

The cost is nothing, until you try to hide from it. It should be an exploration of human honesty, inner freedom, and the silent prisons we build within ourselves. At its core lies a simple but often terrifying truth: liberation begins not in possession, achievement, or external approval, but in the quiet courage to admit to oneself, what is real.

We need to confront the truths long avoided, revealing how denial, pride, and fear cost far more than honesty ever could. We can trace the tension between what we project to the world and what we quietly wrestle with inside.

Ultimately, while admission costs nothing, avoidance extracts everything. To admit is to meet oneself for the first time without disguise. And in that meeting, freedom, raw, uncontrollable, and utterly life-changing, is finally found.

For a very long time, I believed freedom required strength,

certainty, or control. What I did not realize was how much energy I spent avoiding a single act: admitting what was already true. The moment I stopped negotiating with myself, stopped defending narratives that no longer fit, life shifted in ways I could not have predicted.

Admission did not arrive as collapse, but as release. Saying the quiet truths out loud stripped them of their power to haunt me. What I feared would weaken me instead clarified everything. There was no applause, no instant resolution, only a profound lightness where resistance once lived.

After being in constant denial like most, this insight revealed itself when I understood that denial is far more costly than honesty. Admission asks for nothing, yet it returns everything.

> ***'Admission Is Free'***
> *"The single act of 'willing to admit'*
> *will set one free in ways unimaginable."*

Conscious Breather

This explores the transformative power of self-honesty. It reframes admission not as failure or confession, but as liberation from internal resistance. It also affirms that while admission costs nothing, avoidance exacts a heavy toll, and that life changes dramatically the moment truth is acknowledged without disguise or defense.

REFLECTIVE PAUSE: This one may need you to create some extra space. Slow it down a fair bit and notice

```
what you've been avoiding entering. Think about the
truths that were always accessible, yet required
humility rather than effort. The understandings you
postponed because they asked you to arrive without
armor.

Reflect on this carefully: What did you believe
needed to be earned before it could be acknowledged?
Where did pride delay acceptance? If nothing were
demanded of you, what would you finally allow
yourself to see?

Admission asks nothing but honesty. The cost is not
entry, it is surrender. Let this remain present
without resistance. Some doors were never locked,
only ignored. Move ahead with this understanding,
aware that access was never the barrier, readiness
was.
```

Forward Glance

Admission costs nothing, yet it is resisted more fiercely than most sacrifices. The moment truth is acknowledged, effort shifts from defense to release. What once demanded energy to suppress dissolves without struggle. There is no ceremony in admission, no applause, only relief.

And once honesty is chosen without condition, life does not return to what it was before, it moves forward unburdened, lighter for having finally been told the truth.

39

From Doubt to Discovery

Doubt does not arrive by invitation. It forms in the absence of clarity, in the spaces where information is incomplete and understanding feels just out of reach. We carry it with us constantly, often without naming it, allowing it to sit beneath our thoughts like background noise. Because it is familiar, it goes unquestioned.

Over time, doubt becomes a weight on consciousness. It clouds perception, slows decision-making, and subtly shapes the way we interpret experience. Not because it is malicious, but because uncertainty left unattended demands energy. When clarity is missing, the mind fills the gap with hesitation, second-guessing, and imagined outcomes.

Yet doubt is not the enemy it is often made out to be. It is a signal, not a verdict. From doubt to discovery is not a leap of faith, but a movement toward understanding. ***The moment we stop carrying doubt passively and begin engaging with it intentionally, its burden lightens, and what once restricted***

awareness becomes an entry point to insight.

Doubt once felt like an obstacle I needed to overcome. With time, I learned it was a companion, one that arrived not to weaken conviction, but to test its honesty. Every phase of uncertainty carried an invitation to look deeper, to strip away borrowed confidence and sit with what remained.

Discovery did not come through certainty or haste. It emerged slowly, after I stopped rushing answers and allowed doubt to refine my questions. What I found on the other side was not perfection or assurance, but self-trust, a quieter, steadier knowing rooted in experience rather than validation.

This inflection point emerged later in life, when wisdom replaced urgency. Doubt no longer signaled failure, but progress.

> ***'From Doubt to Discovery'***
> *"Only once you remove self-doubt*
> *will you discover self-love*
> *thereby ultimately revealing your true-self."*

Conscious Breather

It explores uncertainty as a necessary passage rather than a flaw. It reframes doubt as a catalyst for self-inquiry that, over time, leads to clarity and self-acceptance. It also affirms that discovery is not immediate, but earned through patience, reflection, and the willingness to move forward without premature certainty.

REFLECTIVE PAUSE: Stop briefly and reconsider your relationship with doubt. Think about the questions you once tried to silence. The uncertainty you treated as weakness instead of invitation.

Reflect on this thoughtfully: When did doubt first appear, and what was it pointing toward? Where did certainty keep you safe, but also still? What became possible the moment you stopped resisting not knowing?

Doubt is not absence of faith. It is often the beginning of discernment. Let this register without urgency. Discovery does not reward those who rush past uncertainty, but those who stay present with it. Carry this with you as you move on, aware that doubt, when met honestly, does not derail the path, it reveals it.

Forward Glance

Doubt does not disappear through certainty, it softens through understanding. What once unsettled begins to guide when questions are allowed to mature without urgency. Discovery arrives quietly, not as proof, but as trust earned over time. When doubt is no longer feared, it becomes an instrument rather than an obstacle.

And in that shift, clarity reveals itself without needing to be forced.

40

When Potential Meets Guidance

Every person is born carrying a gift of some kind, often unremarkable to the world, and sometimes even to themselves. Life rarely creates space for its discovery. Survival, obligation, expectation, and pressure crowd out curiosity, leaving little room to ask who one might become beyond what is required to endure.

Only a small number stumble upon their gift early, sometimes through luck, sometimes through circumstance. For most, it remains dormant until another intervenes, not with instruction, but with recognition. Someone notices what has gone unnamed, articulates it aloud, and in doing so, makes the invisible visible.

Even then, recognition alone is not enough. The rare moment comes when the person hearing it chooses to listen. To believe what they were told. To risk unwrapping what they possess without knowing what it might cost or change. Guidance does not create the gift, but it creates the permission to explore it. And when that permission is accepted, potential begins to move from possibility into form. Potential is often spoken of as something innate, waiting patiently to be claimed.

What I learned over time is that most people cannot access it alone. Not because they lack ability, but because they lack reflection. We rarely see ourselves clearly without another set of eyes willing to look with care. There were moments in my life when someone else recognized a capacity in me before I did. Not through instruction, but through belief, challenge, or simple presence.

Guidance did not create potential, it revealed it. It held a mirror steady long enough for possibility to register. This came from witnessing how often growth accelerates through connection. Potential, left unattended, remains dormant. When met with guidance, it awakens.

> ***'When Potential Meets Guidance'***
> *"Everyone is gifted, but many never unwrap theirs.*
> *Sometimes, it takes another to show them how."*

Conscious Breather

It explores the catalytic role of mentorship and support in personal development. It affirms that potential is real but often unrealized without external insight. It reframes guidance not as control, but as recognition, revealing how belief, challenge, and encouragement can unlock capacities individuals did not yet know they possessed.

```
REFLECTIVE PAUSE: Calm it down and look at the
moments where direction arrived at the right time.
Think about the guidance that didn't create you, but
helped reveal you. The presence that sharpened
potential rather than shaped it.

Reflect on this with clarity: When did guidance
amplify what was already there?  Where did support
strengthen your agency instead of replacing it? How
did you know when it was time to step forward on
your own?

Guidance is most powerful when it recognizes
readiness. It does not lead forever, it prepares.
Let this remain present without attachment. The goal
of guidance is not dependence, but departure. Build
on this as you continue, aware that potential
fulfills itself when guidance knows when to step
aside.
```

Forward Glance

Potential does not announce itself, and it rarely unfolds alone. Most gifts remain dormant not from lack of ability, but from lack of recognition. When another names what we have not yet seen, possibility enters language for the first time. Whether that gift is unwrapped depends on listening, courage, and timing. Guidance does not create potential, it awakens it.

And once awakened, it becomes the responsibility of the one who carries it forward.

IX

Return to Self

After taking 'The Honest Turn' we return to first principles, dismantling illusions of hierarchy, superiority, and inherited authority.
These reflections explore unity, equality, reason, and balance beyond dogma.
Separation dissolves, identity simplifies, and wisdom circles back to wholeness.
Growth here is no longer ascent, but return, a quiet reconciliation with what was always true.
As you enter, consider what you have been taught to elevate, and what may never have been separate at all.

41

The Journey Back to One

As we move through life, we are surrounded by rituals. Each culture offers its own symbols, ceremonies, expectations, and identities to inhabit. We are taught how to celebrate, how to mourn, how to belong, and how to define ourselves within those structures.

Over time, these rituals accumulate, shaping behavior, belief, and self-concept, until identity feels inseparable from what we have been taught to perform.

Yet there is a truth that waits patiently at the end of every journey. When death stands before us, it demands everything be left behind. Titles, roles, allegiances, rituals, and identities lose their meaning in an instant. What remains is not affiliation, but essence. The self, stripped of form, returns to simplicity.

This arose from recognizing that much of life is spent building layers that must eventually be released. The journey back to one is not an erasure, but a reconciliation. A quiet return to what existed before identity was assigned, and what remains when all ceremony falls away.

Life begins in unity, long before language, labels, or division take hold. Over time, we are named, categorized, assigned roles, beliefs, and allegiances, each one pulling us further from simplicity. What starts as expansion slowly becomes fragmentation, until identity feels crowded rather than clear.

I came to see that much of adulthood is spent shedding what was added rather than acquiring something new. Titles fall away. Certainties soften. Attachments loosen. What remains is not emptiness, but coherence. A return to self without performance, without audience, without the need to explain.

This insight stemmed from recognizing that becoming whole is often an act of subtraction. The journey forward eventually circles back.

> ***'The Journey Back to One'***
> *"Ironically, we're all born as one,*
> *baptized into many*
> *and eventually die without any."*

Conscious Breather

It reflects on the natural arc from unity to fragmentation and back again. It reframes growth as a return rather than an ascent, where identity simplifies through unlearning. It also affirms wholeness as a rediscovery of self beneath layers of conditioning, a quiet reconciliation with what existed before division began.

```
REFLECTIVE PAUSE: This one requires you create some
space and allow yourself to arrive. Think about the
moments when complexity fell away and something
essential remained. Not because it was explained,
but because it was felt.

Reflect on this gently: When did you feel most
aligned without trying to be? What parts of you
surfaced when labels, roles, and expectations
loosened? If everything unnecessary were set aside,
what would still feel true?

The journey back is not regression. It is
integration. Let this awareness settle without
nostalgia. Wholeness is not found ahead, it is
remembered. Consider this as you move on, aware that
unity is not something you become, it is something
you return to.
```

Forward Glance

Life moves us through countless identities, rituals, and roles, each borrowed from culture, belief, and circumstance. We carry them proudly, defend them fiercely, and mistake them for who we are. Yet in the final accounting, all distinctions fall away. Death asks for everything to be left behind, name, status, allegiance, and story alike. What remains is not what we accumulated, but what we were beneath it all.

The journey back to one is not a loss of identity, but a return to essence, the quiet recognition that we were never separate to begin with.

42

Equality Beyond Illusion

For centuries, humanity accepted hierarchy as destiny. Kingdoms, monarchies, royal bloodlines, and divine authority ruled unquestioned, shaping societies where power flowed downward and obedience flowed up. These structures were not sustained by strength alone, but by belief. By convincing the many that order required elevation, and that elevation required submission.

As awareness slowly emerged, cracks began to show. People started to see that these systems were less about protection and more about control, carefully designed to keep the balance tilted. The few accumulated excess while the many learned to survive with less, mistaking endurance for fairness. Inequality became normalized, even justified, as tradition or necessity.

Most of these structures have since fallen, not through revolt alone, but through recognition. Yet some remain, preserved by influence, wealth, and the quiet mechanisms of power that adapt faster than resistance. Their persistence is not proof of legitimacy, but of how deeply control embeds itself when left unexamined. Equality, once seen clearly, becomes difficult to unsee.

We sometimes speak of equality as though it is a settled truth, yet continue to organize the world around hierarchy, titles, and inherited authority.

The contradiction is rarely acknowledged. We still praise equal worth in principle, then excuse unequal standing through tradition, divinity, status, or moral elevation.

Over time, I learned to separate rhetoric from reality. If all lives are equal, no crown, doctrine, or claim of superiority can withstand honest scrutiny. Equality does not coexist with exemption. The moment someone is placed above reproach, equality becomes performance rather than principle.

This idea originated from confronting how often equality is invoked selectively. Not to unite, but to comfort. Not to level, but to justify imbalance.

> ***'Equality Beyond Illusion'***
> *"If you believe that all lives matter,*
> *and are created equal, then,*
> *any royalty accession,*
> *claim of divinity*
> *or higher moral authority*
> *is simply unfounded."*

Conscious Breather

It dismantles the false comforts of proclaimed equality that tolerate hierarchy and moral exemption. It challenges inherited authority, divinity claims, and elevated status as contradictions to true equality. It also affirms equality as a lived standard, not a slogan, one that holds only when no one stands above accountability or below dignity.

REFLECTIVE PAUSE: Step back and look past the surface of fairness. Think about the ways equality is spoken about versus how it is practiced. The ideals that sound complete, yet remain uneven in application.

Reflect on this carefully: Where have you benefited from systems you question? When did equality become symbolic rather than lived? What assumptions remain untouched because they appear neutral?

Equality loses meaning when it ignores context. It becomes illusion when it avoids examination. Let this remain present without defensiveness. Seeing clearly does not require guilt, only honesty. Carry this forward as you continue, aware that true equality begins when illusion is dismantled, not defended.

Forward Glance

Hierarchy survives only as long as it is believed. For centuries, kingdoms, monarchies, and inherited power ruled by convincing the many that inequality was order and obedience was destiny. As awareness grows, these structures weaken, not because they are attacked, but because they are seen.

Some still persist, sustained by influence and control rather than legitimacy. Yet once the illusion of superiority dissolves, equality ceases to be an idea and becomes a standard.

And standards, once recognized, are difficult to abandon without conscious denial.

43

Beyond Superiority

Building on the foundation laid in the previous piece of 'Equality Beyond Illusion', this takes another deliberate step in dismantling the grip of the few over the many.

Superiority rarely survives honest examination, yet most people bow to it anyway. Not because they believe in it deeply, but because fear is persuasive.

Fear of consequence, exclusion, punishment, or standing alone. It is easier to submit than to question, easier to revere than to confront the absence of real distinction.

Recognizing no one as superior requires an uncommon level of confidence. Not arrogance, but inner stability.

When you no longer seek permission, approval, or protection, hierarchy loses its grip. Superiority dissolves the moment fear does.

This reflection arose from observing how power sustains itself less through force and more through compliance. The illusion persists only as long as it is obeyed.

> ***'Beyond Superiority'***
> *"It takes an insurmountable*
> *level of confidence to realise*
> *that no being is superior to another."*

Conscious Breather

This examines hierarchy as a construct maintained by fear rather than merit. It reframes equality as an act of courage, requiring the confidence to stand without submission. It also affirms that no being is inherently above another, and that superiority exists only where fear is allowed to replace self-respect.

```
REFLECTIVE PAUSE: Take a moment to examine where
hierarchy still lives. Think about the subtle ways
superiority shows up, in belief, language,
certainty, or dismissal. Not always loudly, often
quietly, dressed as confidence or correctness.

Reflect on this with honesty: Where have you placed
yourself above others without intending to? What did
that position protect you from feeling? How often
has comparison replaced understanding?

Superiority does not strengthen identity. It narrows
it. Let this register without defensiveness.
Releasing the need to be above does not diminish
worth, it restores balance. Hold this as you
continue, aware that clarity deepens when standing
```

```
beside others replaces standing over them.
```

Forward Glance

Superiority endures not because it is true, but because fear keeps it intact. Fear of standing alone, fear of consequence, fear of being cast out for refusing to bow. Yet the moment fear loosens its grip, hierarchy collapses inward. No one stands above another without consent. When self-respect replaces submission, superiority loses its audience.

And without an audience, it cannot survive.

44

Reason Against Dogma

Even today, the world remains scarred by illegitimate wars and conflict zones driven not by necessity, but by belief systems hardened into dogma. Entire populations are conditioned to accept that one truth must dominate another, that righteousness belongs exclusively to one side, one scripture, one interpretation. This conviction does not arise organically. It is cultivated.

Theological dogma, when fused with power and politics, becomes an accelerant. It simplifies complex human realities into absolutes, good and evil, chosen and condemned, justified and expendable. Those at the top wield belief as leverage, while those below are taught to defend narratives that rarely serve them. Control masquerades as faith. Violence is framed as duty.

Reason stands in stark contrast to this cycle. It asks what is being protected, who benefits, and why generations are still being sacrificed to beliefs that refuse examination. These conflicts endure not because they are unsolvable, but because questioning them threatens the structures that depend on perpetual division. Until reason is allowed to challenge dogma without fear, the cost will continue to be paid in human lives, long after the original beliefs have lost their meaning.

Across centuries, dogma has asked for obedience where understanding was inconvenient. ***It offered certainty in exchange for surrender, answers without inquiry, and belonging without thought. Time and again, reason has been positioned as the adversary, not because it is dangerous, but because it refuses to kneel.***

I came to realise that dogma survives by discouraging examination. It divides by declaring itself unquestionable, then sanctifies that division as truth.

Reason, by contrast, does not demand agreement, only engagement. It challenges inherited certainty not to destroy meaning, but to test its integrity.

This reflection emerged from recognizing that progress, moral, social, and intellectual, has always required dissent. Every advance once stood accused of heresy. Reason does not seek to replace belief, but to prevent belief from becoming weaponized.

> ***'Reason Against Dogma'***
> *"Theology by definition, creates divide*
> *and divide, inevitably fuels conflict.*

> *Conflict leads to war,*
> *and war ultimately ends in death.*
> *Submission to a higher intellect,*
> *will challenge you to refute this logic."*

Conscious Breather

This examines the enduring tension between inquiry and unquestioned authority. It traces how dogma has historically resisted scrutiny while reason has driven evolution through challenge and evidence. It also affirms reason as a unifying force, one that confronts division, dismantles false authority, and safeguards humanity from the consequences of blind submission.

REFLECTIVE PAUSE: Step way back and look at what you've defended without revisiting. Think about the beliefs you inherited fully formed. The ideas protected by tradition, repetition, or authority rather than understanding.

Reflect on this with care: When was the last time you questioned something you were taught to revere? Where did loyalty override inquiry? What would change if reason were allowed to sit beside belief?

Dogma resists examination because it fears erosion. Reason invites it because it trusts what remains. Let this remain present without rebellion. Questioning is not betrayal, it is participation. Consider this as you continue, aware that truth does not require protection from thought, it requires honesty within it.

Forward Glance

Dogma endures where questioning is forbidden and belief is weaponized as identity. Even now, wars rage and lives are lost in defense of narratives that refuse examination, sustained by power, politics, and fear rather than truth. Reason threatens these structures not because it destroys meaning, but because it exposes who benefits from blind allegiance. As long as belief is protected from inquiry, conflict remains useful to those who control it.

Reason does not end violence by force, it ends it by removing the illusion that obedience is virtue and division is destiny.

45

Beyond Balance

For years, health was presented to us as something measurable, visible, and narrow. Steps taken, calories counted, hours worked, symptoms treated. Yet the longer I observed human behavior, the clearer it became that well-being extends far beyond the physical body.

We fracture ourselves by tending to one dimension while neglecting the others, then wonder why equilibrium feels so hard to sustain.

The truth is this: You are more than a physical body. You are a system of interwoven parts. And each part deserves care, clarity, and connection. Beyond balance isn't a destination, it's a system. A system designed to go from healing, to growing, balancing, thriving and eventually beyond.

Let's be honest: Most people are struggling. Not because they don't care about their health but because they've been told the wrong version of what "health" even is. ***We've been taught to***

count steps, calories, and hours worked. But no one taught us to measure peace. Or connection. Or self-trust. No one gave us a way to track the health of our relationships, our culture, our finances, our digital boundaries, or our sense of purpose.

So we chase. We grind. We "optimize." And we quietly burn out behind curated highlight reels and half-finished self-help books. Beyond Balance is designed to unlock a new paradigm with 13 Keys to wholeness of wellness. The system blends insight and reflection to help grow, balance, and thrive across body, mind, and spirit.

There are thirteen forms of health that shape the quality of a life, spanning body, mind, and spirit. Most are not hidden or mysterious, they are present in plain sight, woven into how we think, connect, work, relate, and rest. What makes them elusive is not their absence, but our conditioning. We are taught to optimize fragments instead of nurturing the whole.

This contemplation was inspired by recognizing that balance is not a destination, but a living system. When even one form of health is ignored, strain appears elsewhere. True well-being requires awareness, intention, and the willingness to tend to what cannot always be quantified, but is always felt.

> ***'Beyond Balance'***
> *"An absurd fact, is that we are*
> *born with minimal health.*
> *It takes considerable levels*
> *of tolerance of this life*

> *to become immune to the*
> *vulnerabilities of human existence*
> *which can only be conquered with*
> *health of body, mind and spirit."*

Conscious Breather

This reframes health as a multidimensional system requiring conscious care of body, mind, and spirit. It introduces the concept of thirteen interconnected forms of health, many overlooked despite being ever-present. It also affirms that wholeness is achieved not through perfection, but through consistent attention to the full spectrum of human well-being.

The 13 forms of health are interconnected, and balancing them is crucial for conquering holistic health and harmony. Can you name the 13 forms of health needed for balancing health of body, mind and spirit?

REFLECTIVE PAUSE: Take this one in with depth. Stop and reconsider what balance has meant to you. Think about the times you aimed for equilibrium by diminishing yourself. The compromises framed as fairness that quietly asked too much.

Reflect on this thoughtfully: Where did balance become self-negotiation? What did you equalize that was never meant to be equal? How often did you mistake restraint for harmony?

Balance is not always neutral. Sometimes it is avoidance wearing discipline. Let this awareness settle without judgment. Not everything requires symmetry to be right. Know this as you continue, recognizing that balance without honesty cannot last.

Forward Glance

Balance is not something achieved once and kept intact. It is a living relationship between body, mind, and spirit, constantly adjusting as life unfolds. When even one form of health is neglected, strain appears elsewhere, often unnoticed until it demands attention. Wholeness is not found in optimization, but in awareness, in recognizing what needs care before it breaks.

Beyond balance is a way of living that listens inward, responds honestly, and tends to the whole rather than chasing fragments.

Beyond Balance was never intended to remain a single reflection. Instead, its evolution lies in a full-length book by the same title, presented as a practical blueprint for cultivating wellness through wholeness.

This work is accompanied by a dedicated app and an integrated, mind-shifting educational system designed to help individuals understand, assess, and nurture all thirteen forms of health across body, mind, and spirit.

Together, the book, app and system moves beyond theory, offering a living framework that guides awareness into action, and balance into a sustainable way of being rather than a fleeting goal.

X

Living Forward

After we 'Return to Self', we now bring the journey to its most grounded reckoning.
These reflections explore inheritance, dignity, self-preservation, and the constant motion of identity.

Legacy is stripped of illusion, peace is chosen over conflict, and worth reclaimed through sovereignty.
This closing movement affirms becoming as ongoing and freedom as a lived decision.
As you arrive, consider what you are ready to carry forward, and what you are finally willing to leave behind.

46

The Inheritance Burden

Inheritance is rarely received without expectation. Across generations, wealth, land, titles, and control are passed down with the assumption that continuity will preserve stability. Yet more often than not, inheritance becomes a fault line.

Decisions made by the departed, who controls what, who receives how much, who is deemed worthy, frequently ignite division rather than unity. History is crowded with empires that collapsed not from external attack, but from internal expectation. Power concentrates, entitlement grows, and loyalty erodes. Dynasties fracture as successors battle not enemies, but their own.

What was built through sacrifice becomes a battleground for control, and in the aftermath, new empires rise not to honor legacy, but to challenge it. Perhaps the most enduring tragedy lies in the gap between effort and entitlement. Those who sacrificed often believed they were securing a future.

Instead, they left behind assets unaccompanied by discipline, responsibility, or gratitude.

Inheritance without stewardship accelerates decay. What was meant to preserve becomes the very force that dismantles.

I watched people speak endlessly about generational wealth, legacy, about what they would leave behind, as though permanence could be purchased or preserved through accumulation. But after watching an entitled generation rise, I began to question the very notion of inheritance, knowing that within 100 years, none of us alive today will remain.

I came to understand that inheritance is not a gift wrapped in comfort, but a responsibility carried forward. Blood, name, reputation, values, these arrive without consent and endure without escape. They shape how one is received, judged, trusted, or dismissed long before a word is spoken. Unlike wealth, they cannot be spent away or hidden.

This reflection emerged from rejecting the illusion that provision equals preparation. To inherit character is heavier than inheriting currency, because it demands something in return. To whom, then, am I leaving what? Why spend decades building, saving, and denying oneself, for the sake of legacy only to be forgotten within a month?

This is not a declaration of absence. It is not an intention to leave nothing behind. It is an invitation to reconsider what inheritance truly means. ***Beyond possessions, titles, or material security, there is a deeper transfer that shapes a life***

more enduringly. Perspective, values, discernment, resilience, and the courage to think independently are legacies that do not depreciate with time.

What I hope to pass on is not burden, but clarity. Not entitlement, but understanding. If this reflection sparks thought in my own offspring, or in anyone else reading it, then it has served its purpose. Inheritance should not merely provide, it should prepare. And perhaps the most meaningful inheritance is not what is received, but what is awakened.

This awakening compelled me to craft the following letter:

> *"To my offspring,*
>
> *When I go, there will be no fortune*
> *passed down to hasten that moment.*
> *Instead, you will inherit things far more enduring:*
> *my blood that runs through you,*
> *my name that you carry,*
> *my reputation built over time,*
> *my words etched into memory,*
> *and the values I lived by,*
> *whether in silence or defiance.*
>
> *This is your inheritance.*
> *Weighty. Inescapable. Enduring.*
> *Not to burden you but to remind you*
> *that legacy isn't counted in coin,*
> *it is measured in character.*

> *Expect nothing less and no more, so carry it well.*
> *Good luck!*
>
> *Sincerely,*
> *Parent who gave you life*
>
> *P.S. If this isn't sufficient, start building more to leave a generous legacy to your offspring."*

Conscious Breather

It reframes legacy as obligation rather than reward. It challenges the fixation on material inheritance and elevates character, values, and reputation as the true assets passed between generations. It also affirms that what we leave behind is not what we owned, but what others must carry forward, and that the greatest inheritance is not comfort, but responsibility.

REFLECTIVE PAUSE: Did this sink in? Take a moment, pause and reconsider what inheritance truly means. Think about what has been passed down to you, not only materially, but ideologically, emotionally, and behaviorally. The values you absorbed, the fears you inherited, the expectations you carried without question.

Reflect on this with honesty: What did you receive that strengthened you, and what quietly weighed you down? Which beliefs were offered as guidance, and which arrived as obligation? If you were to pass something forward, what would you choose to refine rather than repeat?

Inheritance is not only what is given. It is what is

examined, accepted, transformed, or released. Let this remain present without guilt. Questioning what you inherit is not rejection, it is stewardship. Reflect on this as you continue, aware that the most meaningful legacy is not what you leave behind, but what you teach others to see for themselves.

Forward Glance

Inheritance is rarely neutral. What is passed down carries expectation, control, and unresolved consequence alongside wealth or name. Empires collapse not only through conquest, but through entitlement, division, and the struggle to possess what was never truly owned. Sacrifice made by one generation does not guarantee stewardship by the next. When inheritance is received without responsibility, it accelerates decay rather than continuity.

What endures is not what is claimed, but what is upheld, and legacy survives only where discipline outlives entitlement.

47

Walk Away, Choose You

Confrontation is the daily rhythm of existence, a force we meet headlong without pause for its hidden toll. We charge into it unflinching, yet in that very act, we unwittingly terrorize our own foundations, eroding the quiet stability and self-worth we so desperately need.

Walking away is rarely impulsive. It is usually preceded by long periods of justification, patience, and self-negotiation. We exhaust every internal argument for staying before we ever consider leaving. We tell ourselves it is temporary, that things will change, that endurance is strength. In reality, this delay is often less about hope and more about fear, fear of guilt, fear of judgment, fear of becoming the villain in someone else's story.

This is where choosing yourself feels most uncomfortable. Not because it is wrong, but because it disrupts the identity you have been maintaining. Leaving asks you to disappoint expectations you once upheld, including your own. It forces a reckoning between who you are becoming and who others need you to remain. And in that tension, clarity begins to form, not as certainty, but as relief.

Why aren't we taught from our earliest years that another path exists, one without shame, one that liberates rather than imprisons? Walking away, choosing oneself, would not weaken us; it would forge a more compassionate society, where peace is not won through battle but reclaimed through wisdom.

I took it upon myself to articulate what might be that better way, a deliberate architecture for inner peace that honors the soul's right to preserve itself.

> ***'Walk Away, Choose You'***
> *"If it resembles a battle,*
> *it's not worth the fight.*
> *Peace begins the moment*
> *you choose to walk away*
> *from what doesn't."*

Conscious Breather

Letting go isn't defeat, it's freedom in disguise. This is a compelling meditation on the strength it takes to release what no longer aligns with your peace. It challenges the notion that endurance always equals virtue and redefines walking away, not as giving up, but as an act of radical self-preservation. In a world that glorifies persistence at any cost, pause, reflect, and make the audacious choice to prioritize inner harmony over external validation.

This narrative explores the emotional terrain between conflict and clarity, the place where one realizes that some battles cannot be won without losing oneself. Through philosophical reflection, lived wisdom, and deeply personal insight, true freedom begins not in conquest, but in surrender. It's a glimpse into detachment, courage, and the art of choosing peace even when the ego demands revenge or resolution.

Ultimately, this is not a story about escape, but about return, the quiet homecoming to oneself after years of trying to fix, please, or fight for what was never meant to stay. It is an invitation to choose peace over pride, authenticity over attachment, and the self over the struggle.

For someone anywhere, this could resonate deeply in a fast-paced, often conflict-driven world. It serves as a reminder to seek peace not through winning every fight, but through knowing when to step back and focus on what truly nurtures the soul.

This offers a profound insight into the nature of conflict and peace. It challenges the instinct to fight every battle and instead proposes that true strength lies in the choice to walk away from what doesn't serve us.

While it may not apply universally to every situation, it provides a valuable framework for prioritizing mental and emotional well-being over unnecessary strife.

REFLECTIVE PAUSE: This one could be considered controversial. So, slow it down completely and acknowledge what you already know. Think about the moments you stayed longer than you should have. Not because you were unsure, but because leaving felt heavier than enduring.

Reflect on this honestly: What were you hoping would change if you stayed? How many times did you choose understanding over self-preservation? At what point did loyalty begin to cost you yourself?

Walking away is not abandonment. It is discernment. Let this register without justification. Choosing yourself does not require explanation to those who benefitted from your silence. Take this further as you continue, aware that departure is sometimes the most honest form of alignment.

Forward Glance

Walking away is rarely the first choice, but it is often the clearest one. It comes after effort has been spent, boundaries explained, and hope exhausted. Choosing yourself is not abandonment of others, it is refusal to abandon your own well-being. When staying demands self-erasure, leaving becomes an act of integrity.

And once that choice is made, peace no longer needs permission to follow.

48

Deprivation of Dignity

Beneath the language of civility and progress, humanity still operates by the oldest rule of all, dominance. The law of the jungle never disappeared, it simply learned to dress itself differently.

The lion is king because he is the strongest, and in human systems, strength often takes the form of power, wealth, influence, or force. Those who possess it demand respect not through merit, but through intimidation.

What is rarely acknowledged is the cost of submission. The masses who bow, comply, and internalize hierarchy do not escape unscathed. Each act of enforced reverence inflicts a quiet injury on the psyche.

Over time, self-worth erodes, agency weakens, and stress embeds itself in the body. The demand to honor power simply because it dominates creates trauma that manifests as anxiety, resentment, illness, and disconnection.

This reflection emerged from recognizing that dignity is not taken only through violence, but through normalization. ***When oppression is framed as order and submission as respect, the deepest harm is not physical, it is internal.*** A society that conditions its people to bow teaches them to fracture themselves in order to survive.

This piece emerged later and in the most provocative forms, at a moment when the institutions I once trusted could no longer withstand scrutiny. What had appeared stable began to fracture under examination, and traditions I had accepted without question revealed the cost of their own preservation. The clarity was unsettling, but it was honest.

As my understanding deepened, I began to see how dignity is not always taken through force, but often surrendered through ritual, reverence, and compliance. What is framed as respect can quietly become erasure, and what is called order can mask submission. The most enduring systems do not rely on violence alone, they rely on participation.

This reflection took shape from that reckoning. Not as rebellion, but as refusal. A refusal to trade self-worth for ceremony, authority, or inherited hierarchy, and a recognition that the deepest harm is inflicted when dignity is normalized as something to be bowed away

> ***'Deprivation of Dignity'***
> *"The ultimate trauma*
> *one can inflict on another,*

> *is to deprive them of dignity.*
> *By bowing in the face of authority,*
> *royalty or any figure,*
> *is not submission but the silent theft*
> *of one's own sovereignty,*
> *a ritualized erasure of worth*
> *disguised as respect."*

Conscious Breather

This confronts the subtle mechanisms through which self-worth is surrendered under the guise of respect and tradition. It examines how institutional authority sustains itself through ritualized compliance rather than overt force, reframing dignity as a non-negotiable aspect of human sovereignty. It also challenges normalized hierarchies and calls for conscious resistance to any system that requires self-erasure in exchange for acceptance or order. It's a call to reclaim personal sovereignty.

REFLECTIVE PAUSE: Hold, pause and acknowledge what was diminished. Think about the moments where dignity was compromised slowly, not through a single act, but through repetition, tolerance, or necessity. The times you adjusted yourself to remain acceptable.

Reflect on this carefully: Where did you allow dignity to be negotiated rather than honored? What did you excuse because resistance felt too costly? When did endurance replace self-respect?

Dignity is rarely stripped all at once. It erodes when silence becomes routine. Let this remain

```
present without anger. Recognition is not weakness,
it is reclamation. Move ahead with this
understanding, aware that restoring dignity often
begins with refusing what once felt unavoidable.
```

Forward Glance

When strength is mistaken for worth, dignity becomes negotiable. The powerful demand reverence, the vulnerable learn to bow, and submission is normalized as survival. What is rarely acknowledged is the damage this inflicts inwardly, on health, on identity, on the quiet sense of self that learns to shrink in order to endure. Dignity is not lost in a single act, but eroded through repetition.

And once that erosion is accepted as order, the greatest deprivation is no longer imposed from above, but carried within.

49

The Constant Self in Motion

Each day we wake as someone new, whether we recognize it or not. Experience accumulates quietly overnight, perspective shifts, and the world itself has moved while we slept. Nothing is static. The planet turns, circumstances evolve, and time advances without pause or permission. There is no option to return to who we were yesterday, only the choice of how we meet who we are today.

Progress, in this sense, is unavoidable. Every minute carries us forward, altering context, opportunity, and understanding. What remains within our control is not the movement itself, but our response to it. To resist change is to exhaust oneself against a force that cannot be reversed. To engage with it consciously is to grow alongside it.

This thought emerged as a result of seeing motion not as pressure, but as invitation. ***Each new day offers a chance to step forward with greater awareness, to refine intention, to act with a little more care than before***. Becoming better is not a demand placed upon us, it is a possibility extended daily, simply by choosing how we move.

There was a time when I searched for a fixed version of myself, a point of arrival where identity would settle and remain intact. Life corrected that expectation. What I came to understand is that constancy does not live in stillness, but in motion. Each day offers a subtle renewal, an opportunity to meet oneself again without obligation to who one was yesterday.

Change no longer feels like loss. It feels like honesty. To remain in motion is not instability, it is responsiveness. Growth does not erase continuity, it refines it. What moves forward carries traces of what came before, but is not bound by it. Every morning grants permission to adjust, recalibrate, and reintroduce oneself anew. This thought emerged from accepting that becoming is endless. There is no final self to protect, only a living one to tend.

> ***'The Constant Self in Motion'***
> *"Who I am today, is not who I was yesterday*
> *and definitely not who I will be tomorrow.*
> *Everyday, I have the pleasure of*
> *introducing myself to you, and you,*
> *the option of meeting a new me."*

Conscious Breather

It affirms identity as an evolving process rather than a fixed state. It reframes change as continuity in progress, where renewal is available each day. I aim to close the current journey with acceptance of becoming, honoring movement as the truest expression of self and each forward step as a quiet beginning.

REFLECTIVE PAUSE: Give that a moment to land. Look within and notice what has remained while everything else shifted. Think about the changes you've lived through, roles released, beliefs revised, versions outgrown. Now look at what persisted beneath all that movement.

Reflect on this thoughtfully: What part of you has adapted without disappearing? Where have you mistaken evolution for instability? How has movement refined you rather than scattered you?

Change does not negate continuity. It reveals it. Let this awareness settle without needing definition. You are not inconsistent for evolving, you are coherent in motion. Carry this with you as you continue, aware that becoming is not departure from self, but the way self stays alive.

Forward Glance

Nothing remains as it was, not the world, not the body, not the self. Each day carries us forward by default, shifting context, perspective, and possibility without asking permission. There is no return to who we were yesterday, only the choice of how we meet who we are becoming. Motion is not instability, it is life unfolding. And within that movement lies opportunity, to adjust, to refine, to act with greater awareness than before.

The self remains constant not by standing still, but by continuing forward, consciously, one day at a time.

50

The Rude Awakening

To bring this reflection to a pause, though the journey itself knows no end, I aim to leave you with a map of seven levels of consciousness, reimagined so you may discern where you stand and where your truth resides.

Then, ascend with awareness, and move forward with intention. We pause not because the journey ends, but because reflection deepens in stillness.

Let us rest here, if only for a moment, knowing that awakening has no final destination. ***Consider the seven levels of consciousness, reframed to help you recognize your current horizon and the one that calls you next.*** Step forward, deliberately, with purpose.

I offer you these levels of consciousness as a mirror, to see where you are, where you belong, and how you might rise beyond. Move onward, with intention as your guide.

> ***The Art of Waking Up'***
> *"The world does not awaken us.*
> *Consciousness appears the moment*
> *we stop outsourcing our thinking."*

Humanity does not awaken all at once. Consciousness unfolds in layers, like a flower responding to light, each petal opening only when it is ready. Most never move beyond the first layer. Not out of failure, but out of comfort.

The Comfortable Dream:

Level One is where the majority remain, dreaming within the dream, mistaking routine for purpose, obedience for identity, and repetition for life. Here, the world is accepted as it is presented. The system is mistaken for destiny. The script is followed without question, because questioning feels unsafe.

This framing of consciousness is not hierarchy for the sake of superiority. It is orientation. Without a map, growth feels like chaos. Without language, awakening feels isolating. To level up requires first understanding where one stands.

The First Fracture:

The Second Level begins with a quiet discomfort. A subtle fracture forms between what is lived and what is felt. Days repeat, yet something rings hollow. You sense that life, as performed, is not life as lived. This is not rebellion. It is recognition. A private knowing that something essential is missing.

Borrowed Truths:

At the Third Level, inquiry takes form. The sacred structures of belief are no longer immune to examination. Religion, politics, culture, even science are questioned, not to dismantle them recklessly, but to understand their limits. Authority loses its automatic credibility. Truth is no longer inherited, it is pursued.

Cognitive Dissonance:

The Fourth Level reveals the architecture beneath the surface. You begin to see how fear is manufactured, how attention is harvested, how distraction replaces meaning. Control becomes visible, not as a villain, but as a system sustained by participation. Blame fades. Responsibility turns inward. You recognize that the most effective prison was always internal.

Radical Self-Responsibility:

At the Fifth Level, awareness shifts from structure to energy. Emotion is no longer random. Thought is no longer harmless. You see how inner states shape outer experience. Gratitude replaces acquisition. Presence replaces ambition. Creation becomes conscious.

Integrated Awareness:

The Sixth Level brings an unmistakable clarity. Salvation was never external. No institution, no ideology, no figure was coming to complete you. The divine spark you sought has been quietly guiding you all along. Separation dissolves. Meaning simplifies.

Conscious Choice:

The Seventh Level is not escape, but embodiment. You live awake in a world still asleep, grounded without being bound. The world may feel smaller now, less fitting, not because it diminished, but because you expanded. The higher your awareness, the less illusion can contain you.

This work was never meant to offer answers, only mirrors. What you have encountered here is not a doctrine to adopt, but a series of reflections shaped by unlearning, confrontation, and quiet resolve. If it has unsettled you at moments, that is not an accident. Discomfort is often the first signal that something true has brushed against us.

It's is a record of a mind choosing awareness over autopilot, integrity over inheritance, and freedom over conformity. Its fragments were written not to persuade, but to provoke reflection, to loosen the grip of borrowed beliefs, and to remind us that sovereignty begins the moment we stop outsourcing our thinking.

Distilled down to its deepest spine, the recurring truth here can be: ***freedom is not something we acquire, it is something we remember once we stop outsourcing thought, identity, and authority.***

The truth beneath it was never about agreement. It was about permission. Permission to think freely, live deliberately, and walk your own path without needing it to be understood.

While the seven-level consciousness model is not a formal

psychological theory, it aligns with many contemporary psychological ideas about growth, self-awareness, and the evolution of consciousness. It can be seen as a reflective, practical companion to established psychological frameworks, offering a roadmap for personal development that resonates with, but does not duplicate mainstream psychological models.

'The Art of Waking Up' began as a solitary contemplation but has grown into something far more expansive: a full-length book titled: "The Rude Awakening" that functions as a practical roadmap for navigating the seven levels of consciousness.

Supporting this foundation is a comprehensive course designed to guide individuals through each level methodically-building understanding, enabling self-assessment, and fostering genuine cultivation of consciousness. Together, they form a complete system for mastering 'The 7 Leveles of Consciousness - The Art of Waking Up'.

Conclusion: The Ongoing Becoming

I did not write to please, reassure, or soften the edges of thought. These pages exist to interrupt automatic understanding, to challenge inherited reflexes, and to quietly reprogram the way conscious awareness awakens to itself.

If discomfort appears here, it is not accidental, it is a signal. Awakening rarely arrives through affirmation alone, it begins when familiar frameworks are questioned and attention is returned to what has long been overlooked.

This work closes not with answers, but with honesty and was never meant to be definitive, orderly, or resolved. It exists as it was lived, unfiltered in its questioning, unbound by expectation, and unlearned in its willingness to dismantle what once felt certain.

These reflections were not written to instruct, persuade, or impress, but to observe, confront, and release. What remains is not a conclusion in the traditional sense, but a confirmation: that growth does not require polish, truth does not need permission, and consciousness, when left unscripted, reveals more than any carefully rehearsed narrative ever could.

The more the world fractures into extremes, left and right,

reason and reaction, noise and certainty, the more I have learned to trust the stillness within. Not because I stand above it, but because I no longer feel compelled to stand inside it. The distance that once felt like loneliness now feels like clarity. What drifted away did so because it could not travel this far inward.

Along this journey, I've come to realise that I am no longer concerned with fitting in. ***I have no appetite for borrowed beliefs, inherited outrage, or applause that requires self-erasure. I have my own mind, my own moral compass, and a conscience that answers inward, not upward.*** Those who meet me briefly will form their conclusions.

Those who know me deeply will recognize the continuity beneath the change. Both perceptions can coexist without conflict.

And so, the shadow of rejection no longer holds its claim, because I understand now that most rejection is merely misalignment wearing a louder voice. Validation from a world that misunderstands itself is not a prize worth winning. What matters is coherence, between thought and action, values and behavior, intention and impact.

What follows from here is not continuation on the page, but in practice. In how you listen, what you tolerate, where you draw boundaries, and which inner voice you choose to trust when no one is watching. Growth rarely announces itself. It unfolds quietly, through small, courageous acts of honesty repeated over time.

Where this journey has led me, it has done so through the full spectrum of emotion that time allows. Joy and grief, certainty and doubt, belonging and isolation have each left their mark. Yet I arrive without regret and without resentment.

What remains is gratitude for having been allowed to walk this far with eyes open, to gather insight rather than armor, and to carry forward not conclusions, but the hope that wisdom will continue to light whatever path unfolds next.

To those who catalyzed growth, some who shaped love, the many who challenged the real me, anchored me, softened me, and stood firm beside me in both fracture and becoming, know this: your influence is woven into every page, every insight, every evolution. You did not simply walk alongside me, you altered the trajectory of my life. In ways visible and unseen, you gave these words permission to exist.

Whatever else may change, time, places, relationships, even the person I am still growing into, you all remain part of the unshakable core I return to. For walking with me through the pivotal moments and the ordinary days alike, you have my enduring gratitude and a place in my story that no one else can ever replace. All of you, your presence awakened something in me that had been asleep for far too long.

There were days I genuinely doubted I'd make it to where I stand now, and others where I still fail to notice the distance I've already crossed. That blind spot is human, but the gratitude that breaks through it feels like something else entirely. I can only credit consciousness: the quiet witness that keeps me moving, and then reminds me, when I forget, that I did.

If there is anything these pages ask of you, it is not agreement, but courage. The courage to question what you inherited. To release what no longer fits. To walk away when peace demands it. To stand alone when integrity requires it. And to return, again and again, to yourself without apology.

If these words have given language to something you already felt but could not yet name, then they have served their purpose. And if they have challenged you, let that challenge remain alive. Sit with it. Question it. Make it your own, or discard it entirely.

This is not the end of becoming. It is simply your beginning, a breath taken with awareness. Consciousness does not conclude, it continues. And if you find something of yourself reflected here, then this work has already done what it was meant to do.

Go gently, this is not an ending.
It is the ongoing becoming.

Epilogue: Upon Arrival

There's a quiet gravity to someone who knows who they are. Not the loud kind, not the performative kind, not the "watch me" kind. The kind you feel before they even speak, because nothing about them is reaching for permission. They don't need to win the room. They don't need to shrink for it either. They simply arrive as themselves, and that steadiness does something to the air around them.

It's tempting to call that "confidence," but confidence can be borrowed. It can be a good outfit, a practiced tone, a well timed laugh. Knowing who you are is different. It isn't decoration, it's alignment. It's the inner agreement that says, "This is what I stand for, this is what I won't trade, and this is what I'm still learning."

The irony is that this kind of self knowing rarely comes from certainty. It comes from contact. From being tested by life and noticing what remains true when your plans don't. From saying yes when you mean yes, and learning to say no without turning it into a speech. From getting it wrong, admitting it, and realizing your identity didn't collapse just because your ego did.

People who know who they are don't feel the need to narrate it. You can spot them by what they don't do. ***They don't fish for validation with every sentence. They don't weaponize their success. They don't confuse being misunderstood with being profound. They don't turn every disagreement into a referendum on their worth.*** They can hold their own opinions without making them everyone else's burden.

And maybe that's why it's attractive, because it's rare. Most of us spend years performing pieces of ourselves like a patchwork resume: the version that gets accepted, the version that gets praised, the version that keeps the peace. We become fluent in adapting, but forget how to return. We learn how to be impressive before we learn how to be honest.

Knowing who you are isn't a finish line. It's a practice. A daily act of remembering. You don't "find yourself" once and then keep yourself forever. You meet yourself again and again, in different seasons, under different pressures, with different stakes. The goal isn't to stay the same. The goal is to stay true, even as you change.

Sometimes self knowing looks like ambition. Sometimes it looks like rest. Sometimes it looks like walking away from what everyone else would chase. Sometimes it looks like starting over without making a martyrdom out of it. Sometimes it looks like doing the quiet thing that's right, when the loud thing would get you applause.

If there's any final thread worth carrying forward, it's this: the world has endless opinions about who you should be, but your life gets easier the moment you stop outsourcing that job.

So don't rush to define yourself with labels you haven't earned through lived experience. Don't let a single chapter of your life claim the whole book. Pay attention to what enlarges you, what drains you, what you keep returning to when you're alone and no one is watching. Let your decisions reveal you, because they will, whether you're intentional or not.

And when you do begin to know who you are, hold it gently. Not as a trophy, but as a compass. Not as a reason to feel above anyone, but as a reason to stop abandoning yourself.

Because the most attractive thing isn't perfection. It's presence. It's the calm courage of someone who has met themselves, made peace with what they found, and keeps choosing to live from that place.

The finish line is for the ego. The journey is for the soul.
Think deeply, and above all, live unscripted!
Keep going...

Afterword: The Point of No Return

The scariest part of awakening is not what you discover, it's what you lose the ability to pretend. Because once something in you opens, it doesn't politely close again. ***You can't unsee what you've seen. You can't unknow what your body now recognizes as truth.*** And from that moment on, the old version of you, the one who could tolerate what felt misaligned, starts to feel like a coat you've outgrown while still wearing it.

That's when the shaking begins. ***Awakening doesn't just change your thoughts, it changes your standards.*** It changes what you can participate in without paying for it internally. And so, life starts requesting edits.

Some relationships have to change, not always because people become "bad," but because the contract was written by an earlier you. A fear-based you. A you that needed approval more than peace. When you awaken, you stop negotiating with your own intuition. You stop shrinking to keep dynamics intact. You may find yourself craving honesty over harmony, depth over familiarity, and that alone can rearrange an entire circle.

Your work can change too. Not necessarily overnight, not always dramatically, but unmistakably. ***What once felt impres-***

sive might start feeling empty. What once felt secure might start feeling suffocating. You begin to sense the cost of living out of alignment, the invisible tax of performing a life that no longer fits. And you start asking different questions, not "How do I succeed?" but "What am I serving, and is it worthy of me?"

Even your passions evolve. The things you chased for validation lose their flavor. The things you dismissed as "impractical" start calling you home. ***You may grieve the old hunger, the old urgency, the old identity that knew exactly how to be rewarded.*** But what replaces it is quieter and far more powerful: a desire that comes from within, not from lack.

Why does all of this happen? Because awakening is spiritual. It is the slow exit from a third-dimensional version of yourself, the version built mainly from conditioning, survival, and fear. ***It's the shift from living by the mind's control to living by the heart's truth.*** And yes, that is terrifying, because it threatens the entire architecture of the life you constructed while you were still trying to stay safe.

You don't just change habits, you change gravity. And in that shift, it can feel like everything is falling apart. But often, what's actually happening is something more honest: what was built on fear can no longer hold you.

If you're in that place right now, the in-between, the unraveling, the "I don't recognize myself" phase, I want you to hear this clearly: you are not breaking. You are becoming incompatible with what was never meant to be permanent.

You have the courage for this, even if your nervous system disagrees at the moment.

Healing will ask you to release control. The mind will fight this, the ego will negotiate, the past will offer you familiar discomfort as if it's a gift. But the more you heal, the more you let go, the more you loosen the grip of the old strategies, the more you can finally hear what's been true beneath the noise: your intuition was never absent, it was simply outvoted.

As you return to your heart, you return to your power. Not the loud kind. Not the performative kind. The kind that doesn't need permission. The kind that chooses peace without explaining itself. The kind that says "no" without hatred and "yes" without fear.

And then something beautiful happens. ***Life becomes more abundant, not because you forced it, but because you stopped resisting it.*** It becomes easier, not because nothing is hard, but because you are no longer at war with your own knowing. It moves with more flow, not because you controlled every outcome, but because you released what was blocking you: the need to remain who you were.

Awakening is the moment you realize you can't go back. Not as punishment, as proof. Proof that something real has begun. Proof that you're done living half-alive. Proof that the life ahead of you requires the new you, and the new you is not a stranger, it's your original self, finally allowed to lead.

So let the fear speak, then let it pass. ***Let what no longer serves you fall away, even if it leaves silence at first.*** Step into the new life gently, bravely, imperfectly, but consciously.

You don't need to have it all figured out.
You only need to keep choosing what's true.
Because, once you've seen it, you can't unsee it...

Front Cover: Synopsis

The book cover depicts a disconnected light bulb to illustrate the ***radical concept of self-generated consciousness***, suggesting that true awareness does not require external permission or traditional power sources.

By presenting a glow that exists independently of wires or switches, the imagery emphasizes that ***enlightenment is an internal awakening*** rather than a gift bestowed by authority.

The surrounding darkness serves as a quiet stage for this ***unscripted presence***, highlighting a mind that has moved from inherited narratives toward personal clarity.

Ultimately, the synopsis serves to frame the book as a call to ***courageous autonomy***, where the individual discovers they are capable of finding meaning without relying on prescribed societal structures.

About the Author

Aryan Costa is a writer, creator and systems thinker whose work explores the inner architecture of a meaningful life: identity, integrity, and the quiet choices that shape who we become. With a voice that blends philosophical reflection and practical clarity, he writes for who are tired of borrowed beliefs and ready to live with intention.

His work sits at the intersection of self inquiry and real world application, translating introspection into usable frameworks that support growth, resilience, and personal sovereignty. Whether he is examining conscience, relationships, or the myths we inherit, his aim is consistent: to help people see themselves more honestly, then move through life with greater coherence.

Aryan's writing is both mirror and compass, grounded, unfiltered, and ultimately devoted to freedom that can be lived, not just admired. He invites you to question with courage, rebuild with intention, and live with a kind of alignment that doesn't need constant noise to feel real.